No and Yes, Pulpit and Press, Retrospection and Introspection, Rudimental Divine Science, and Unity of Good

by

Mary Baker Eddy

The Echo Library 2007

Published by

The Echo Library

Echo Library
131 High St.
Teddington
Middlesex TW11 8HH

www.echo-library.com

Please report serious faults in the text to complaints@echo-library.com

ISBN 978-1-40685-005-5

NO AND YES

PULPIT AND PRESS.

RETROSPECTION AND INTROSPECTION

RUDIMENTAL DIVINE SCIENCE

UNITY OF GOOD

by

MARY BAKER EDDY

4

CONTENTS

NO AND YES

PREFACE

It was the purpose of each edition of this pamphlet to benefit no favored class, but, according to the apostle's admonition, to "reprove, rebuke, exhort," and with the power and self-sacrificing spirit of Love to correct involuntary as well as voluntary error.

By a modification of the language, the import of this edition is, we trust, transparent to the hearts of all conscientious laborers in the realm of Mind-healing. To those who are athirst for the life-giving waters of a true divinity, it saith tenderly, "Come and drink;" and if you are babes in Christ, leave the meat and take the unadulterated milk of the Word, until you grow to apprehend the pure spirituality of Truth.

MARY BAKER EDDY

NO AND YES

INTRODUCTION

To kindle in all minds a common sentiment of regard for the spiritual idea emanating from the infinite, is a most needful work; but this must be done gradually, for Truth is as "the still, small voice," which comes to our recognition only as our natures are changed by its silent influence.

Small streams are noisy and rush precipitately; and babbling brooks fill the rivers till they rise in floods, demolishing bridges and overwhelming cities. So men, when thrilled by a new idea, are sometimes impatient; and, when public sentiment is aroused, are liable to be borne on by the current of feeling. They should then turn temporarily from the tumult, for the silent cultivation of the true idea and the quiet practice of its virtues. When the noise and stir of contending sentiments cease, and the flames die away on the mount of revelation, we can read more clearly the tablets of Truth.

The theology and medicine of Jesus were one,—in the divine oneness of the trinity, Life, Truth, and Love, which healed the sick and cleansed the sinful. This trinity in unity, correcting the individual thought, is the only Mind-healing I vindicate; and on its standard have emblazoned that crystallized expression, CHRISTIAN SCIENCE.

A spurious and hydra-headed mind-healing is naturally glared at by the pulpit, ostracized by the medical faculty, and scorned by people of common sense. To aver that disease is normal, a God-bestowed and stubborn reality, but that you can heal it, leaves you to work against that which is natural and a law of being. It is scientific to rob disease of all reality; and to accomplish this, you cannot begin by admitting its reality. Our Master taught his students to deny self, sense, and take up the cross. Mental healers who admit that disease is real should be made to test the feasibility of what they say by healing one case audibly, through such an admission,—if this is possible. I have healed more disease by the spoken than the unspoken word.

The honest student of Christian Science is modest in his claims and conscientious in duty, waiting and working to mature what he has been taught. Institutes furnished with such teachers are becoming beacon-lights along the shores of erudition; and many who are not teachers have large practices and some marked success in healing the most defiant forms of disease.

Dishonesty destroys one's ability to heal mentally. Conceit cannot avert the effects of deceit. Taking advantage of the present ignorance in relation to Christian Science Mind-healing, many are flooding our land with conflicting theories and practice. We should not spread abroad patchwork ideas that in some vital points lack Science. How sad it is that envy will bend its bow and shoot its arrow at the idea which claims only its inheritance, is naturally modest, generous, and sincere! while the trespassing error murders either friend or foe who stands in its way. Truly it is better to fall into the hands of God, than of man.

When I revised "Science and Health with Key to the Scriptures," in 1878, some irresponsible people insisted that my manual of the practice of Christian Science Mind-healing should not be made public; but I obeyed a diviner rule. People dependent on the rules of this practice for their healing, not having lost the Spirit which sustains the genuine practice, will put that book in the hands of their patients, whom it will heal, and recommend it to their students, whom it would enlighten. Every teacher must pore over it in secret, to keep himself well informed. The Nemesis of the history of Mind-healing notes this hour.

Dishonesty necessarily stultifies the spiritual sense which Mind-healers specially need; and which they must possess, in order to be safe members of the community. How good and pleasant a thing it is to seek not so much thine own as another's good, to sow by the wayside for the way-weary, and trust Love's recompense of love.

Plagiarism from my writings is so common it is becoming odious to honest people; and such compilations, instead of possessing the essentials of Christian Science, are tempting and misleading.

Reading Science and Health has restored the sick to health; but the task of learning thoroughly the Science of Mind-healing and demonstrating it understandingly had better be undertaken in health than sickness.

DISEASE UNREAL

Disease is more than *imagination*; it is a human error, a constituent part of what comprise the whole of mortal existence,—namely, material sensation and mental delusion. But an erring sense of existence, or the error of belief, named disease, never made sickness a stubborn reality. On the ground that harmony is the truth of being, the Science of Mind-healing destroys the feasibility of disease; hence error of thought becomes fable instead of fact. Science demonstrates the reality of Truth and the unreality of the error. A self-evident proposition, in the Science of Mind-healing, is that disease is unreal; and the efficacy of my system, beyond other systems of medicine, vouches for the validity of that statement. Sin and disease are not scientific, because they embody not the idea of divine Principle, and are not the phenomena of the immutable laws of God; and they do not arise from the divine consciousness and true constituency of being.

The unreality of sin, disease, and death, rests on the exclusive truth that being, to be eternal, must be harmonious. All disease must be—and can only be—healed on this basis. All true Christian Scientists are vindicating, fearlessly and honestly, the Principle of this grand verity of Mind-healing.

In erring mortal thought the reality of Truth has an antipode,—the reality of error; and disease is one of the severe realities of this error. God has no opposite in Science. To Truth there is no error. As Truth alone is real, then it follows that to declare error real would be to make it Truth. Disease arises from a false and material sense, from the belief that matter has sensation. Therefore this material sense, which is untrue, is of necessity unreal. Moreover, this unreal sense substitutes for Truth an unreal belief,—namely, that life and health are independent of God, and dependent on material conditions. Material sense also avers that Spirit, or Truth, cannot restore health and perpetuate life, but that material conditions can and do destroy both human health and life.

If disease is as real as health, and is itself a state of being, and yet is arrayed against being, then Mind, or God, does not meddle with it. Disease becomes indeed a stubborn reality, and man is mortal. A "kingdom divided against itself is brought to desolation;" therefore the mind that attacks a normal and real condition of man, is profanely tampering with the realities of God and His laws. Metaphysical healing is a lost jewel in this misconception of reality. Any contradictory fusion of Truth with error, in both theory and practice, prevents one from healing scientifically, and makes the last state of one's patients worse than the first. If disease is real it is not illusive, and it certainly would contradict the Science of Mind-healing to attempt to destroy the realities of Mind in order to heal the sick.

On the theory that God's formations are spiritual, harmonious, and eternal, and that God is the only creator, Christian Science refutes the validity of the testimony of the senses, which take cognizance of their own phenomena,— sickness, disease, and death. This refutation is indispensable to the destruction of false evidence, and the consequent cure of the sick,—as all understand who practise the true Science of Mind-healing. If, as the error indicates, the evidence of disease is not false, then disease cannot be healed by denying its validity; and this is why the mistaken healer is not successful, trying to heal on a material basis.

The evidence that the earth is motionless and the sun revolves around our planet, is as sensible and real as the evidence for disease; but Science determines the evidence in both cases to be unreal. To material sense it is plain also that the error of the revolution of the sun around the earth is more apparent than the adverse but true Science of the stellar universe. Copernicus has shown that what appears real, to material sense and feeling, is absolutely unreal. Astronomy, optics, acoustics, and hydraulics are all at war with the testimony of the physical senses. This fact intimates that the laws of Science are mental, not material; and Christian Science demonstrates this.

SCIENCE OF MIND-HEALING

The rule of divinity is golden; to be wise and true rejoices every heart. But evil influences waver the scales of justice and mercy. No personal considerations should allow any root of bitterness to spring up between Christian Scientists, nor cause any misapprehension as to the motives of others. We must love our enemies, and continue to do so unto the end. By the love of God we can cancel error in our own hearts, and blot it out of others.

Sooner or later the eyes of sinful mortals must be opened to see every error they possess, and the way out of it; and they will "flee as a bird to your mountain," away from the enemy of sinning sense, stubborn will, and every imperfection in the land of Sodom, and find rescue and refuge in Truth and Love.

Every loving sacrifice for the good of others is known to God, and the wrath of man cannot hide it from Him. God has appointed for Christian Scientists high tasks, and will not release them from the strict performance of each one of them. The students must now fight their own battles. I recommend that Scientists draw no lines whatever between one person and another, but think, speak, teach, and write the truth of Christian Science without reference to right or wrong personality in this field of labor. Leave the distinctions of individual character and the discriminations and guidance thereof to the Father, whose wisdom is unerring and whose love is universal.

We should endeavor to be long-suffering, faithful, and charitable with all. To this small effort let us add one more privilege—namely, silence whenever it can substitute censure. Avoid voicing error; but utter the truth of God and the beauty of holiness, the joy of Love and "the peace of God, that passeth all understanding," recommending to all men fellowship in the bonds of Christ. Advise students to rebuke each other always in love, as I have rebuked them. Having discharged this duty, counsel each other to work out his own salvation, without fear or doubt, knowing that God will make the wrath of man to praise Him, and that the remainder thereof He will restrain. We can rejoice that every germ of goodness will at last struggle into freedom and greatness, and every sin will so punish itself that it will bow down to the commandments of Christ,— Truth and Love.

I enjoin it upon my students to hold no controversy or enmity over doctrines and traditions, or over the misconceptions of Christian Science, but to work, watch, and pray for the amelioration of sin, sickness, and death. If one be found who is too blind for instruction, no longer cast your pearls before this state of mortal mind, lest it turn and rend you; but quietly, with benediction and hope, let the unwise pass by, while you walk on in equanimity, and with increased power, patience, and understanding, gained from your forbearance. This counsel is not new, as my Christian students can testify; and if it had been heeded in times past it would have prevented, to a great extent, the factions which have sprung up among Scientists to the hindrance of the Cause of Truth. It is true that the mistakes, prejudices, and errors of one class of thinkers must not be introduced or established among another class who are clearer and more conscientious in their convictions; but this one thing can be done, and should be: let your opponents alone, and use no influence to prevent their legitimate action from their own standpoint of experience, knowing, as you should, that God will well regenerate and separate wisely and finally; whereas you may err in effort, and lose your fruition.

Hoping to pacify repeated complaints and murmurings against too great leniency, on my part, towards some of my students who fall into error, I have opposed occasionally and strongly—especially in the first edition of this little work—existing wrongs of the nature referred to. But I now point steadfastly to the power of grace to overcome evil with good. God will "furnish a table in the wilderness" and show the power of Love.

Science is not the shibboleth of a sect or the cabalistic insignia of philosophy; it excludes all error and includes all Truth. More mistakes are made in its name than this period comprehends. Divinely defined, Science is the atmosphere of God; humanly construed, and according to Webster, it is "knowledge, duly arranged and referred to general truths and principles on which it is founded, and from which it is derived." I employ this awe-filled word in both a divine and human sense; but I insist that Christian Science is demonstrably as true, relative to the unseen verities of being, as any proof that can be given of the completeness of Science.

The two largest words in the vocabulary of thought are "Christian" and "Science." The former is the highest style of man; the latter reveals and interprets God and man; it aggregates, amplifies, unfolds, and expresses the ALL-God. The life of Christ is the predicate and postulate of all that I teach, and there is but one standard statement, one rule, and one Principle for all scientific truth.

My hygienic system rests on Mind, the eternal Truth. What is termed matter, or relates to its so-called attributes, is a self-destroying error. When a so-called material sense is lost, and Truth restores that lost sense,—on the basis that all consciousness is Mind and eternal,—the former position, that sense is organic and material, is proven erroneous.

The feasibility and immobility of Christian Science unveil the true idea,— namely, that earth's discords have not the reality of Mind in the Science of being; and this idea—dematerializing and spiritualizing mortals—turns like the needle to the pole all hope and faith to God, based as it is on His omnipotence and omnipresence.

Eternal harmony, perpetuity, and perfection, constitute the phenomena of being, governed by the immutable and eternal laws of God; whereas matter and human will, intellect, desire, and fear, are not the creators, controllers, nor destroyers of life or its harmonies. Man has an immortal Soul, a divine Principle, and an eternal being. Man has perpetual individuality; and God's laws, and their intelligent and harmonious action, constitute his individuality in the Science of Soul.

In its literary expression, my system of Christian metaphysics is hampered by material terms, which must be used to indicate thoughts that are to be understood metaphysically. As a Science, this system is held back by the common ignorance of what it is and what it does, and (worse still) by those who come falsely in its name. To be appreciated, Science must be understood and conscientiously introduced. If the Bible and Science and Health had the place in schools of learning that physiology occupies, they would revolutionize and reform the world, through the power of Christ. It is true that it requires more study to understand and demonstrate what these works teach, than to learn theology, physiology, or physics; because they teach divine Science, with fixed Principle, given rule, and unmistakable proof.

Ancient and modern human philosophy are inadequate to grasp the Principle of Christian Science, or to demonstrate it. Revelation shows this Principle, and will rescue reason from the thrall of error. Revelation must subdue the sophistry of intellect, and spiritualize consciousness with the dictum and the demonstration of Truth and Love. Christian Science Mind-healing can only be gained by working from a purely Christian standpoint. Then it heals the sick and exalts the race. The essence of this Science is right thinking and right acting—leading us to see spirituality and to be spiritual, to understand and to demonstrate God.

The Massachusetts Metaphysical College and Church of Christ, Scientist, in Boston, were the outgrowth of the author's religious experience. After a lifetime of orthodoxy on the platform of doctrines, rites, and ceremonies, it became a sacred duty for her to impart to others this new-old knowledge of God.

The same affection, desire, and motives which have stimulated true Christianity in all ages, and given impulse to goodness, in or out of the Church, have nerved her purpose to build on the new-born conception of the Christ, as Jesus declared himself,—namely, "the way, the truth, and the life." Living a true life, casting out evil, healing the sick, and preaching the gospel of Truth,—these are the ends of Christianity. This divine way impels a spiritualization of thought and method, beyond doctrine and ritual; and in nothing else has she departed from the old landmarks.

The unveiled spiritual signification of the Word so enlarges our sense of God that it makes both sense and Soul, man and Life, immaterial, though still individual. It removes all limits from divine power. God must be found all instead of a part of being, and man the reflection of His power and goodness. This Science rebukes sin with its own nothingness, and thus destroys sin quickly and utterly. It makes disease unreal, and this heals it.

The demonstration of moral and physical growth, and a scientific deduction from the Principle of all harmony, declare both the Principle and idea to be divine. If this be true, then death must be swallowed up in Life, and the prophecy of Jesus fulfilled, "Whosoever liveth and believeth in me shall never die." Though centuries passed after those words were originally uttered, before this reappearing of Truth, and though the hiatus be longer still before that saying is demonstrated in Life that knows no death, the declaration is nevertheless true, and remains a clear and profound deduction from Christian Science.

IS CHRISTIAN SCIENCE OF THE SAME LINEAGE AS SPIRITUALISM OR THEOSOPHY?

Science is not susceptible of being held as a mere theory. It is hoary with time. It takes hold of eternity, voices the infinite, and governs the universe. No greater opposites can be conceived of, physically, morally, and spiritually, than Christian Science, spiritualism, and theosophy.

Science and Health has effected a revolution in the minds of thinkers on the subject of mediumship, and given impulse to reason and revelation, goodness and virtue. A theory may be sound in spots, and sparkle like a diamond, while other parts of it have no lustre. Christian Science is sound in every part. It is neither warped nor misconceived, when properly demonstrated. If a spiritualist medium understood the Science of Mind-healing, he would know that between those who have and those who have not passed the transition called death, there can be no interchange of consciousness, and that all sensible phenomena are merely subjective states of mortal mind.

Theosophy is a corruption of Judaism. This corruption had a renewal in the Neoplatonic philosophy; but it sprang from the Oriental philosophy of Brahmanism, and blends with its magic and enchantments. Theosophy is no more allied to Christian Science than the odor of the upas-tree is to the sweet breath of springtide, or the brilliant coruscations of the northern sky are to solar heat and light.

IS CHRISTIAN SCIENCE FROM BENEATH, AND NOT FROM ABOVE?

Hear the words of our Master: "Go ye into all the world"! "Heal the sick, cast out devils"! Christian Scientists, perhaps more than any other religious sect, are obeying these commands; and the injunctions are not confined to Jesus' students in that age, but they extend to this age,—to as many as shall believe on him. The demand and example of Jesus were not from beneath. Are frozen dogmas, persistent persecution, and the doctrine of eternal damnation, from above? Are the dews of divine Truth, falling on the sick and sinner, to heal them, from beneath? "By their fruits ye shall know them."

Reading my books, without prejudice, would convince all that their purpose is right. The comprehension of my teachings would enable any one to prove these books to be filled with blessings for the whole human family. Fatiguing Bible translations and voluminous commentaries are employed to explain and prop old creeds, and they have the civil and religious arms in their defense; then why should not these be equally extended to support the Christianity that heals the sick? The notions of personality to be found in creeds are far more mystic than Mind-healing. It is no easy matter to believe there are three persons in one person, and that one person is cast out of another person. These conceptions of Deity and devil presuppose an impotent God and an incredible Satan.

IS CHRISTIAN SCIENCE PANTHEISTIC?

Christian Science refutes pantheism, finds Spirit neither in matter nor in the modes of mortal mind. It shows that matter and mortal mind have neither origin nor existence in the eternal Mind. Thinking otherwise is what estranges mortals from divine Life and Love. God is All-in-all. He is Spirit; and in nothing is He unlike Himself. Nothing that "worketh or maketh a lie" is to be found in the divine consciousness. For God to know, is to be; that is, what He knows must truly and eternally exist. If He knows matter, and matter can exist in Mind, then mortality and discord must be eternal. He is Mind; and whatever He knows is made manifest, and must be Truth.

If God knows evil even as a false claim, this knowledge would manifest evil in Him and proceeding from Him. Christian Science shows that matter, evil, sin, sickness, and death are but negations of Spirit, Truth, and Life, which are positives that cannot be gainsaid. The subjective states of evil, called mortal mind or matter, are negatives destitute of time and space; for there is none beside God or Spirit and the idea of Spirit.

This infinite logic is the infinite light,—uncomprehended, yet forever giving forth more light, because it has no darkness to emit. Mortals do not understand the All; hence their inference of some other existence beside God and His true likeness,—of something unlike Him. He who is All, understands all. He can have no knowledge or inference but His own consciousness, and can take in no more than all.

The mists of matter—sin, sickness, and death—disappear in proportion as mortals approach Spirit, which is the reality of being. It is not enough to say that matter is the substratum of evil, and that its highest attenuation is mortal mind; for there is, strictly speaking, *no* mortal mind. Mind is immortal. Death is the consequent of an antecedent false assumption of the realness of something unreal, material, and mortal. If God knows the antecedent, He must produce its consequences. From this logic there is no escape. Matter, or evil, is the absence of Spirit or good. Their nothingness is thus proven; for God is good, ever-present, and All.

"In Him we live, and move, and have our being;" consequently it is impossible for the true man—who is a spiritual and individual being, created in the eternal Science of being—to be conscious of aught but good. God's image and likeness can never be less than a good man; and for man to be more than God's likeness is impossible. Man is the climax of creation; and God is not without an ever-present witness, testifying of Himself. Matter, or any mode of mortal mind, is neither part nor parcel of divine consciousness and God's verity.

In Science there is no fallen state of being; for therein is no inverted image of God, no escape from the focal radiation of the infinite. Hence the unreality of error, and the truth of the Scripture, that there is "none beside Him." If mortals could grasp these two words *all* and *nothing*, this mystery of a God who has no knowledge of sin would disappear, and the eternal, infinite harmony would be fathomed. If God could know a false claim, false knowledge would be a part of His consciousness. Then evil would be as real as good, sickness as real as health, death as real as Life; and sickness, sin, and death would be as eternal as God.

IS CHRISTIAN SCIENCE BLASPHEMOUS?

Blasphemy has never diminished sin and sickness, nor acknowledged God in all His ways. Blasphemy rebukes not the godless lie that denies Him as All-in-all, nor does it ascribe to Him all presence, power, and glory. Christian Science does this. If Science lacked the proof of its origin in God, it would be self-destructive, for it rests alone on the demonstration of God's supremacy and omnipotence. Right thinking and right acting, physical and moral harmony, come with Science, and the secret of its presence lies in the universal need of better health and morals.

Human theories, when weighed in the balance, are found unequal to the demonstration of divine Life and Love; and their highest endeavors are, to divine Science, what a child's love of pictures is to art. A child, in his ignorance, may imagine the face of Dante to be the rapt face of Jesus. Thus falsely may the human conceive of the Divine. If the schoolmaster is not Christ, the school gets things wrong, and knows it not; but the teacher is morally responsible.

Good health and a more spiritual religion are the common wants; and these wants have wrought this moral result,—that the so-called mortal mind asks for what Mind alone can supply. This demand militates against the so-called demands of matter, and regulates the present high premium on Mind-healing. If the uniform moral and spiritual, as well as physical, effects of Christian Science were lacking, the premium would go down. That it continues to rise, and the demand to increase, shows its real value to the race. Even doctors will agree that infidelity, ignorance, and quackery have never met the growing wants of humanity. Christian Science is no "Boston craze;" it is the sober second thought of advancing humanity.

IS THERE A PERSONAL DEITY?

God is infinite. He is neither a limited mind nor a limited body. God is Love; and Love is Principle, not person. What the person of the infinite is, we know not; but we are gratefully and lovingly conscious of the fatherliness of this Supreme Being. God is individual, and man is His individualized idea. While material man and the physical senses receive no spiritual idea, and feel no sensation of divine Love, spiritual man and his spiritual senses are drinking in the nature and essence of the individual infinite. A sinful sense is incompetent to understand the realities of being,—that Life is God, and that man is in His image and likeness. A sinner can take no cognizance of the noumenon or the phenomena of Spirit; but leaving sin, sense rises to the fulness of the stature of man in Christ.

Person is formed after the manner of mortal man, so far as he can conceive of personality. Limitless personality is inconceivable. His person and perfection are neither self-created, nor discerned through imperfection; and of God as a person, human reason, imagination, and revelation give us no knowledge. Error would fashion Deity in a manlike mould, while Truth is moulding a Godlike man.

When the term divine Principle is used to signify Deity it may seem distant or cold, until better apprehended. This Principle is Mind, substance, Life, Truth, Love. When understood, Principle is found to be the only term that fully conveys the ideas of God,—one Mind, a perfect man, and divine Science. As the divine Principle is comprehended, God's omnipotence and omnipresence will dawn on mortals, and the notion of an everywhere-present body—or of an infinite Mind starting from a finite body, and returning to it—will disappear.

Ever-present Love must seem ever absent to ever-present selfishness or material sense. Hence this asking amiss and receiving not, and the common idolatry of man-worship. In divine Science, God is recognized as the only power, presence, and glory.

Adam's mistiness and Satan's reasoning, ever since the flood,—when specimens of every kind emerged from the ark,—have run through the veins of all human philosophy. Human reason is a blind guide, a continued series of mortal hypotheses, antagonistic to Revelation and Science. It is continually straying into forbidden by-paths of sensualism, contrary to the life and teachings of Jesus and Paul, and the vision of the Apocalypse. Human philosophy has ninety-nine parts of error to the one-hundredth part of Truth,—an unsafe decoction for the race. The Science that Jesus demonstrated, whose views of Truth Confucius and Plato but dimly discerned, Science and Health interprets. It was not a search after wisdom; it was wisdom, and it grasped in spiritual law the universe,—all time, space, immortality, thought, extension. This Science demonstrated the Principle of all phenomena, identity, individuality, law; and showed man as reflecting God and the divine capacity. Human philosophy would dethrone perfection, and substitute matter and evil for divine means and ends.

Human philosophy has an undeveloped God, who unfolds Himself through material modes, wherein the human and divine mingle in the same realm and consciousness. This is rank infidelity; because by it we lose God's ways and perpetuate the supposed power and reality of evil *ad infinitum*. Christian Science rends this veil in the pantheon of many gods, and reproduces the teachings of Jesus, whose philosophy is incontestable, bears the strain of time, and brings in the glories of eternity; "for other foundation can no man lay than that is laid, which is Jesus Christ."

Divine philosophy is demonstrably the true idea of the Christ, wherein Principle heals and saves. A philosophy which cannot heal the sick has little resemblance to Science, and is, to say the least, like a cloud without rain, "driven about by every wind of doctrine." Such philosophy has certainly not touched the hem of the Christ garment.

Leibnitz, Descartes, Fichte, Hegel, Spinoza, Bishop Berkeley, were once clothed with a "brief authority;" but Berkeley ended his metaphysical theory with a treatise on the healing properties of tar-water, and Hegel was an inveterate snuff-taker. The circumlocution and cold categories of Kant fail to improve the conditions of mortals, morally, spiritually, or physically. Such miscalled metaphysical systems are reeds shaken by the wind. Compared with the inspired wisdom and infinite meaning of the Word of Truth, they are as moonbeams to the sun, or as Stygian night to the kindling dawn.

IS THERE A PERSONAL DEVIL?

No man hath seen the person of good or of evil. Each is greater than the corporeality we behold.

"He cast out *devils*." This record shows that the term devil is generic, being used in the plural number. From this it follows that there is more than one devil. That Jesus cast several persons out of another person, is not stated, and is impossible. Hence the passage must refer to the *evils* which were cast out.

Jesus defined devil as a mortal who is full of evil. "Have I not chosen you twelve, and one of you *is a devil?*" His definition of evil indicated his ability to cast it out. An incorrect concept of the nature of evil hinders the destruction of evil. To conceive of God as resembling—in personality, or form—the personality that Jesus condemned as devilish, is fraught with spiritual danger. Evil can neither grasp the prerogative of God nor make evil omnipotent and omnipresent.

Jesus said to Peter, "Get thee behind me, Satan;" but he to whom our Lord gave the keys of the kingdom could not have been wholly evil, and therefore was not a *devil*, after the accepted definition. Out of the Magdalen, Jesus cast seven devils; but not one person was named among them. According to Crabtre, these devils were the diseases Jesus cast out.

The most eminent divines, in Europe and America, concede that the Scriptures have both a literal and a moral meaning. Which of the two is the more important to gain,—the literal or the moral sense of the word *devil*,—in order to cast out this devil? Evil is a quality, not an individual.

As mortals, we need to discern the claims of evil, and to fight these claims, not as realities, but as illusions; but Deity can have no such warfare against Himself. Knowledge of a man's physical personality is not sufficient to inform us as to the amount of good or evil he possesses. Hence we cannot understand God or man, through the person of either. God is All-in-all; but He is definite and individual, the omnipresent and omniscient Mind; and man's individuality is God's own image and likeness,—even the immeasurable idea of divine Mind. In the Science of good, evil loses all place, person, and power.

According to Spinoza's philosophy God is amplification. He is in all things, and therefore He is in evil in human thought. He is extension, of whatever character. Also, according to Spinoza, man is an animal vegetable, developed through the lower orders of matter and mortal mind. All these vagaries are at variance with my system of metaphysics, which rests on God as One and All, and denies the actual existence of both matter and evil. According to false philosophy and scholastic theology, God is three persons in one person. By the same token, evil is not only as real as good, but much more real, since evil subordinates good in personality.

The claims of evil become both less and more in Christian Science, than in human philosophies or creeds: *more*, because the evil that is hidden by dogma and human reason is uncovered by Science; and *less*, because evil, being thus uncovered, is found out, and exposure is nine points of destruction. Then appears the grand verity of Christian Science: namely, that evil has no claims and was never a claimant; for behold evil (or devil) is, as Jesus said, "a murderer from the beginning, and the truth abode not in him."

There was never a moment in which evil was real. This great fact concerning all error brings with it another and more glorious truth, that good is supreme. As there is none beside Him, and He is all good, there can be no evil. Simply uttering this great thought is not enough! We must live it, until God becomes the All and Only of our being. Having won through great tribulation this cardinal point of divine Science, St. Paul said, "But now we are delivered from the law, that being dead wherein we were held; that we should serve in newness of spirit, and not in the oldness of the letter."

IS MAN A PERSON?

Man is more than physical personality, or what we cognize through the material senses. Mind is more than matter, even as the infinite idea of Truth is beyond a finite belief. Man outlives finite mortal definitions of himself, according to a law of "the survival of the fittest." Man is the eternal idea of his divine Principle, or Father. He is neither matter nor a mode of mortal mind, for he is spiritual and eternal, an immortal mode of the divine Mind. Man is the image and likeness of God, coexistent and coeternal with Him.

Man is not absorbed in Deity; for he is forever individual; but what this everlasting individuality is, remains to be learned. Mortals have not seen it. That which is born of the flesh is not man's eternal identity. Spiritual and immortal man alone is God's likeness, and that which is mortal is not man in a spiritually scientific sense. A material, sinful mortal is but the counterfeit of immortal man.

The mind-quacks believe that mortal man is identical with immortal man, and that the immortal is inside the mortal; that good and evil blend; that matter and Spirit are one; and that Soul, or Spirit, is subdivided into spirits, or souls,— *alias* gods. This infantile talk about Mind-healing is no more identical with Christian Science than the babe is identical with the adult, or the human belief resembles the divine idea. Hence it is impossible for those holding such material and mortal views to demonstrate my metaphysics. Theirs is the sensuous thought, which brings forth its own sensuous conception. Mine is the spiritual idea which transfigures thought.

All real being represents God, and is in Him. In this Science of being, man can no more relapse or collapse from perfection, than his divine Principle, or Father, can fall out of Himself into something below infinitude. Man's real ego, or selfhood, is goodness. If man's individuality were evil, he would be annihilated, for evil is self-destroying.

Man's individual being must reflect the supreme individual Being, to be His image and likeness; and this individuality never originated in molecule, corpuscle, materiality, or mortality. God holds man in the eternal bonds of Science,—in the immutable harmony of divine law. Man is a celestial; and in the spiritual universe he is forever individual and forever harmonious. "If God so clothe the grass of the field, ... shall He not much more clothe you, O ye of little faith?"

Sin must be obsolete,—dust returning to dust, nothingness to nothingness. Sin is not Mind; it is but the supposition that there is more than one Mind. It issues a false claim; and the claim, being worthless, is in reality no claim whatever. Matter is not Mind, to claim aught; but Mind is God, and evil finds no place in good. When we get near enough to God to see this, the springtide of Truth in Christian Science will burst upon us in the similitude of the Apocalyptic pictures. No night will be there, and there will be no more sea. There will be no need of the sun, for Spirit will be the light of the city, and matter will be proved a myth. Until centuries pass, and this vision of Truth is fully interpreted by divine Science, this prophecy will be scoffed at; but it is just as veritable now as it can be then. Science, divine Science, presents the grand and eternal verities of God and man as the divine Mind and that Mind's idea.

Mortal man is the antipode of immortal man, and the two should not be confounded. Bishop Foster said, in a lecture in Boston, "No man living hath yet seen man." This material sinful personality, which we misname man, is what St. Paul terms "the old man and his deeds," to be "put off."

Who can say what the absolute personality of God or man is? Who living hath seen God or a perfect man? In presence of such thoughts take off thy shoes and tread lightly, for this is holy ground. Surely the probation of mortals must go on after the change called death, that they may learn the definition of immortal being; or else their present mistakes would extinguish human existence. How long this false sense remains after the transition called death, no mortal knoweth; but this is sure, that the mists of error, sooner or later, will melt in the fervent heat of suffering, mortality will burst the barriers of sense, and man be found perfect and eternal. Of his intermediate conditions—the purifying processes and terrible revolutions necessary to effect this end—I am ignorant.

Inasmuch as these momentous facts in the Science of being must be learned some time, now is the most acceptable time for beginning the lesson. If Science is pointing the way, and is found to bring with it health, holiness, and immortality, then to-day is none too soon for entering this path. The proof that Christian Science is the way of salvation given by Christ, I consider well established. The present, as well as the future, reveals the fact that Truth is never understood too soon.

Has Truth, as demonstrated by Jesus, reappeared? Study Christian Science and practise it, and you will know that Truth has reappeared. What is demonstrably true cannot be gainsaid; but getting the letter and omitting the spirit of this Science is neither the comprehension of its Principle nor the practice of its Life.

HAS MAN A SOUL?

The Scriptures inform us that "the soul that sinneth, it shall die." Here *soul* means sense and organic life; and this passage refers to the Jewish law, that a mortal should be put to death for his own sin, but not for another's. Not Soul, but mortal sense, sins and dies. Immortal man has immortal Soul and a deathless sense of being. Mortal man has but a false sense of Soul and body. He believes that Spirit, or Soul, exists in matter. This is pantheism, and is not the Science of Soul. The mind-quacks have so slight a knowledge of Soul that they believe material and sinning sense to be soul; and then they doctor this soul as if it were not even a material sense.

In Dr. Gordon's sermon on The Ministry of Healing, he said, "The forgiven soul in a sick body is not half a man." Is this pantheistic statement sound theology,—that Soul is in matter, and the immortal part of man a sinner? Is not this a disparagement of the person of man and a denial of God's power? Better far that we impute such doctrines to mortal opinion than to the divine Word.

To my sense, such a statement is a shocking reflection on the divine power. A mortal pardoned by God is not sick, he is made whole. He in whom sin, disease, and death are destroyed, is more than a fraction of himself. Such sermons, though clad in soft raiment, are spiritless waifs, literary driftwood on the ocean of thought; while Truth walks triumphantly over the waves of sin, sickness, and death.

The law of Life and Truth is the law of Christ, destroying all sense of sin and death. It does more than forgive the false sense named sin, for it pursues and punishes it, and will not let sin go until it is destroyed,—until nothing is left to be forgiven, to suffer, or to be punished. Forgiven thus, sickness and sin have no relapse. God's law reaches and destroys evil by virtue of the allness of God.

He need not know the evil He destroys, any more than the legislator need know the criminal who is punished by the law enacted. God's law is in three words, "I am All;" and this perfect law is ever present to rebuke any claim of another law. God pities our woes with the love of a Father for His child,—not by becoming human, and knowing sin, or naught, but by removing our knowledge of what is not. He could not destroy our woes totally if He possessed any knowledge of them. His sympathy is divine, not human. It is Truth's knowledge of its own infinitude which forbids the genuine existence of even a claim to error. This knowledge is light wherein there is no darkness,—not light holding darkness within itself. The consciousness of light is like the eternal law of God, revealing Him and nothing else.

Sympathy with sin, sorrow, and sickness would dethrone God as Truth, for Truth has no sympathy for error. In Science, the cure of the sick demonstrates this grand verity of Christian Science, that you cannot eradicate disease if you admit that God sends it or sees it. Material and mortal mind-healing (so-called) has for ages been a pretender, but has not healed mortals; and they are yet sick and sinful.

Disease and sin appear to-day in subtler forms than they did yesterday. They progress and will multiply into worse forms, until it is understood that disease and sin are unreal, *unknown* to Truth, and never actual persons or real facts.

Our phraseology varies. To me *divine pardon* is that divine presence which is the sure destruction of sin; and I insist on the destruction of sin as the only full proof of its pardon. "For this purpose the Son of God was manifested, that he might *destroy* the works of the devil" (1 John iii. 8).

Jesus cast out evils, mediating between what is and is not, until a perfect consciousness is attained. He healed disease as he healed sin; but he treated them both, not as in or of matter, but as mortal beliefs to be exterminated. Physical and mental healing were one and the same with this master Metaphysician. If the evils called sin, sickness, and death had been forgiven in the generally accepted sense, they would have returned, to be again forgiven; but Jesus said to disease: "Come out of him, and enter no more into him." He said also: "If a man keep my saying, he shall never see death;" and "Whatsoever thou shalt bind on earth shall be bound in heaven." The misinterpretation of such passages has retarded the progress of Christianity and the spiritualization of the race.

A magistrate's pardon may encourage a criminal to repeat the offense; because *forgiveness*, in the popular sense of the word, can neither extinguish a crime nor the motives leading to it. The belief in sin—its pleasure, pain, or power—must suffer, until it is self-destroyed. "Whatsoever a man soweth, that shall he also reap."

IS THERE ANY SUCH THING AS SIN?

Frequently when I touch this subject my meaning is ignorantly or maliciously misconstrued. Christian Science Mind-healing lifts with a steady arm, and cleaves sin with a broad battle-axe. It gives the lie to sin, in the spirit of Truth; but other theories make sin true. Jesus declared that the devil was "a liar, and the father of it." A lie is negation,—*alias* nothing, or the opposite of something. Good is great and real. Hence its opposite, named *evil*, must be small and unreal. When this sense is attained, we shall no longer be the servants of sin, and shall cease to love it.

The domination of good destroys the sense of evil. To illustrate: It seems a great evil to belie and belittle Christian Science, and persecute a Cause which is healing its thousands and rapidly diminishing the percentage of sin. But reduce this evil to its lowest terms, *nothing*, and slander loses its power to harm; for even the wrath of man shall praise Him. The reduction of evil, in Science, gives the dominance to God, and must lead us to bless those who curse, that thus we may overcome evil with good.

If the Bible and my work Science and Health had their rightful place in schools of learning, they would revolutionize the world by advancing the kingdom of Christ. It requires sacrifice, struggle, prayer, and watchfulness to understand and demonstrate what these volumes teach, because they involve divine Science, with fixed Principle, a given rule, and unmistakable proof.

IS THERE NO SACRIFICIAL ATONEMENT?

Self-sacrifice is the highway to heaven. The sacrifice of our blessed Lord is undeniable, and it was a million times greater than the brief agony of the cross; for that would have been insufficient to insure the glory his sacrifice brought and the good it wrought. The spilling of human blood was inadequate to represent the blood of Christ, the outpouring love that sustains man's at-one-ment with God; though shedding human blood brought to light the efficacy of divine Life and Love and its power over death. Jesus' sacrifice stands preeminently amidst physical suffering and human woe. The glory of human life is in overcoming sickness, sin, and death. Jesus suffered for all mortals to bring in this glory; and his purpose was to show them that the way out of the flesh, out of the delusion of all human error, must be through the baptism of suffering, leading up to health, harmony, and heaven.

We shall leave the ceremonial law when we gain the truer sense of following Christ in spirit, and we shall no longer venture to materialize the spiritual and infinite meaning and efficacy of Truth and Love, and the sacrifice that Jesus made for us, by commemorating his death with a material rite. Jesus said: "The hour cometh, and now is, when the true worshippers shall worship the Father in spirit and in truth." They drink the cup of Christ and are baptized in the purification of persecution who discern his true merit,—the unseen glory of suffering for others. Physical torture affords but a slight illustration of the pangs which come to one upon whom the world of sense falls with its leaden weight in the endeavor to crush out of a career its divine destiny.

The blood of Christ speaketh better things than that of Abel. The real atonement—so infinitely beyond the heathen conception that God requires human blood to propitiate His justice and bring His mercy—needs to be understood. The real blood or Life of Spirit is not yet discerned. Love bruised and bleeding, yet mounting to the throne of glory in purity and peace, over the steps of uplifted humanity,—this is the deep significance of the blood of Christ. Nameless woe, everlasting victories, are the blood, the vital currents of Christ Jesus' life, purchasing the freedom of mortals from sin and death.

This blood of Jesus is everything to human hope and faith. Without it, how poor the precedents of Christianity! What manner of Science were Christian Science without the power to demonstrate the Principle of such Life; and what hope have mortals but through deep humility and adoration to reach the understanding of this Principle! When human struggles cease, and mortals yield lovingly to the purpose of divine Love, there will be no more sickness, sorrow, sin, and death. He who pointed the way of Life conquered also the drear subtlety of death.

It was not to appease the wrath of God, but to show the allness of Love and the nothingness of hate, sin, and death, that Jesus suffered. He lived that we also might live. He suffered, to show mortals the awful price paid by sin, and how to avoid paying it. He atoned for the terrible unreality of a supposed existence apart from God. He suffered because of the shocking human idolatry that presupposes Life, substance, Soul, and intelligence in matter,—which is the antipode of God, and yet governs mankind. The glorious truth of being— namely, that God is the only Mind, Life, substance, Soul—needs no reconciliation with God, for it is one with Him now and forever.

Jesus came announcing Truth, and saying not only "the kingdom of God is at hand," but "the kingdom of God is within you." Hence there is no sin, for God's kingdom is everywhere and supreme, and it follows that the human kingdom is nowhere, and must be *unreal*. Jesus taught and demonstrated the infinite as one, and not as two. He did not teach that there are two deities,—one infinite and the other finite; for that would be impossible. He knew God as infinite, and therefore as the All-in-all; and we shall know this truth when we awake in the divine likeness. Jesus' true and conscious being never left heaven for earth. It abode forever above, even while mortals believed it was here. He once spoke of himself (John iii. 13) as "the Son of man which is in heaven,"— remarkable words, as wholly opposed to the popular view of Jesus' nature.

The real Christ was unconscious of matter, of sin, disease, and death, and was conscious only of God, of good, of eternal Life, and harmony. Hence the human Jesus had a resort to his higher self and relation to the Father, and there could find rest from unreal trials in the conscious reality and royalty of his being,—holding the mortal as unreal, and the divine as real. It was this retreat from material to spiritual selfhood which recuperated him for triumph over sin, sickness, and death. Had he been as conscious of these evils as he was of God, wherein there is no consciousness of human error, Jesus could not have resisted them; nor could he have conquered the malice of his foes, rolled away the stone from the sepulchre, and risen from human sense to a higher concept than that in which he appeared at his birth.

Mankind's concept of Jesus was a babe born in a manger, even while the divine and ideal Christ was the Son of God, spiritual and eternal. In human conception God's offspring had to grow, develop; but in Science his divine nature and manhood were forever complete, and dwelt forever in the Father. Jesus said, "Ye do err, not knowing the Scriptures, nor the power of God." Mortal thought gives the eternal God and infinite consciousness the license of a short-lived sinner, to begin and end, to know both evil and good; when evil is temporal and God is eternal,—and when, as a sphere of Mind, He cannot know beginning or end.

The spiritual interpretation of the vicarious atonement of Jesus, in Christian Science, unfolds the full-orbed glory of that event; but to regard this wonder of glory, this most marvellous demonstration, as a personal and material bloodgiving—or as a proof that sin is known to the divine Mind, and that what is unlike God demands His continual presence, knowledge, and power, to meet and master it—would make the atonement to be less than the *at-one-ment*, whereby the work of Jesus would lose its efficacy and lack the "signs following."

From Genesis to Revelation the Scriptures teach an infinite God, and none beside Him; and on this basis Messiah and prophet saved the sinner and raised the dead,—uplifting the human understanding, buried in a false sense of being.

Jesus rendered null and void whatever is unlike God; but he could not have done this if error and sin existed in the Mind of God. What God knows, He also predestinates; and it must be fulfilled. Jesus proved to perfection, so far as this could be done in that age, what Christian Science is to-day proving in a small degree,—the falsity of the evidence of the material senses that sin, sickness, and death are sensible claims, and that God substantiates their evidence by knowing their claim. He established the only true idealism on the basis that God is All, and He is good, and good is Spirit; hence there is no intelligent sin, evil *mind* or matter: and this is the only true philosophy and realism. This divine mystery of godliness was the rock of Truth, on which he built his Church of the new-born, against which the gates of hell cannot prevail.

This Truth is the rock which the builders rejected; but "the same is become the head of the corner." This is the chief corner-stone, the basis and support of creation, the interpreter of one God, the infinity and unity of good.

In proportion as mortals approximate the understanding of Christian Science, they take hold of harmony, and material incumbrance disappears. Having one God, one Mind, one consciousness,—which includes only His own nature,—and loving your neighbor as yourself, constitute Christian Science, which must demonstrate the nothingness of any other state or stage of being.

IS THERE NO INTERCESSORY PRAYER?

All prayer that is desire is intercessory; but kindling desire loses a part of its purest spirituality if the lips try to express it. It is a truism that we can think more lucidly and profoundly than we can write or speak. The silent intercession and unvoiced imploring is an honest and potent prayer to heal and save. The audible prayer may be offered to be heard of men, though ostensibly to catch God's ear,—after the fashion of Baal's prophets,—by speaking loud enough to be heard; but when the heart prays, and not the lips, no dishonesty or vanity influences the petition.

Prophet and apostle have glorified God in secret prayer, and He has rewarded them openly. Prayer can neither change God, nor bring His designs into mortal modes; but it can and does change our modes and our false sense of Life, Love, and Truth, uplifting us to Him. Such prayer humiliates, purifies, and quickens activity, in the direction that is unerring.

True prayer is not asking God for love; it is learning to love, and to include all mankind in one affection. Prayer is the utilization of the love wherewith He loves us. Prayer begets an awakened desire to be and do good. It makes new and scientific discoveries of God, of His goodness and power. It shows us more clearly than we saw before, what we already have and are; and most of all, it shows us what God is. Advancing in this light, we reflect it; and this light reveals the pure Mind-pictures, in silent prayer, even as photography grasps the solar light to portray the face of pleasant thought.

What but silent prayer can meet the demand, "Pray without ceasing"? The apostle James said: "Ye ask, and receive not, because ye ask amiss, to consume it on your lusts." Because of vanity and self-righteousness, mortals seek, and expect to receive, a material sense of approval; and they expect also what is impossible,—a material and mortal sense of spiritual and immortal Truth.

It is sometimes wise to hide from dull and base ears the pure pearls of awakened consciousness, lest your pearls be trampled upon. Words may belie desire, and pour forth a hypocrite's prayer; but thoughts are our honest conviction. I have no objection to audible prayer of the right kind; but the inaudible is more effectual.

I instruct my students to pursue their mental ministrations very sacredly, and never to touch the human thought save to issues of Truth; never to trespass mentally on individual rights; never to take away the rights, but only the wrongs of mankind. Otherwise they forfeit their ability to heal in Science. Only when sickness, sin, and fear obstruct the harmony of Mind and body, is it right for one mind to meddle with another mind, and control aright the thought struggling for freedom.

It is Truth and Love that cast out fear and heal the sick, and mankind are better because of this. If a change in the religious views of the patient comes with the change to health, our Father has done this; for the human mind and body are made better only by divine influence.

SHOULD CHRISTIANS BEWARE OF CHRISTIAN SCIENCE?

History repeats itself. The Pharisees of old warned the people to beware of Jesus, and contemptuously called him "this fellow." Jesus said, "For which of these works do ye stone me?" as much as to ask, Is it the work most derided and envied that is most acceptable to God? Not that he would cease to do the will of his Father on account of persecution, but he would repeat his work to the best advantage for mankind and the glory of his Father.

There are sinners in all societies, and it is vain to look for perfection in churches or associations. The life of Christ is the perfect example; and to compare mortal lives with this model is to subject them to severe scrutiny. Without question, the subtlest forms of sin are trying to force the doors of Science and enter in; but this white sanctuary will never admit such as come to steal and to rob. Through long ages people have slumbered over Christ's commands, "Go ye into all the world, and preach the gospel;" "Heal the sick, cast out devils;" and now the Church seems almost chagrined that by new discoveries of Truth sin is losing prestige and power.

The Rev. Dr. A.J. Gordon, a Boston Baptist clergyman, said in a sermon: "The prayer of faith shall save the sick, and it is doing it to-day; and as the faith of the Church increases, and Christians more and more learn their duty to believe all things written in the Scriptures, will such manifestations of God's power increase among us." Such sentiments are wholesome avowals of Christian Science. God is not unable or unwilling to heal, and mortals are not compelled to have other gods before Him, and employ material forms to meet a mental want. The divine Spirit supplies all human needs. Jesus said to the sick, "Thy sins are forgiven thee; rise up and walk!" God's pardon is the destruction of all "the ills that flesh is heir to."

All power belongs to God; and it is not in all the vain power of dogma and philosophy to dispossess the divine Mind of healing power, or to cast out error with error, even in the name and for the sake of Christ, and so heal the sick. While Science is engulfing error in bottomless oblivion, the material senses would enthrone error as omnipotent and omnipresent, with power to determine the fact and fate to being. It is said that the devil is the ape of God. The lie of evil holds its own by declaring itself both true and good. The path of Christian Science is beset with false claimants, aping its virtues, but cleaving to their own vices. Denial of the authorship of "Science and Health with Key to the Scriptures" would make a lie the author of Truth, and so make Truth itself a lie.

A distinguished clergyman came to be healed. He said: "I am suffering from nervous prostration, and have to eat beefsteak and drink strong coffee to support me through a sermon." Here a skeptic might well ask if the atonement had lost its efficacy for him, and if Christ's power to heal was not equal to the power of daily meat and drink. The power of Truth is not contingent on matter. Our Master said, "Come unto me, all ye that labor and are heavy laden, and I will give you rest." Truth rebukes error; and whether stall-fed or famishing, theology needs Truth to stimulate and sustain a good sermon.

A lady said: "Only He who knows all things can estimate the good your books are doing."

A distinguished Doctor of Divinity said: "Your book leavens my sermons."

The following extract from a letter is a specimen of those received daily: "Your book Science and Health is healing the sick, binding up the broken-hearted, preaching deliverance to the captive, convicting the infidel, alarming the hypocrite, and quickening the Christian."

Christian Science Mind-healing is dishonored by those who take it up from mercenary motives, for wealth and fame, or think to build a baseless fabric of their own on another's foundation. They cannot put the "new wine into old bottles;" they can never engraft Truth into error. Such students come to my College to learn a system which they go away to disgrace. Stealing or garbling my statements of Mind-science will never prevent or reconstruct the wrecks of "*isms*" and help humanity.

Science often suffers blame through the sheer ignorance of people, while envy and hatred bark and bite at its heels. A man's inability to heal, on the Principle of Christian Science, substantiates his ignorance of its Principle and practice, and incapacitates him for correct comment. This failure should make him modest.

Christian Science involves a new language, and a higher demonstration of medicine and religion. It is the "new tongue" of Truth, having its best interpretation in the power of Christianity to heal. My system of Mind-healing swerves not from the highest ethics and from the spiritual goal. To climb up by some other way than Truth is to fall. Error has no hobby, however boldly ridden or brilliantly caparisoned, that can leap into the sanctum of Christian Science.

In Queen Elizabeth's time Protestantism could sentence men to the dungeon or stake for their religion, and so abrogate the rights of conscience and choke the channels of God. Ecclesiastical tyranny muzzled the mouth lisping God's praise; and instead of healing, it palsied the weak hand outstretched to God. Progress, legitimate to the human race, pours the healing balm of Truth and Love into every wound. It reassures us that no Reign of Terror or rule of error will again unite Church and State, or re-enact, through the civil arm of government, the horrors of religious persecution.

The Rev. S.E. Herrick, a Congregational clergyman of Boston, says: "Heretics of yesterday are martyrs to-day." In every age and clime, "On earth peace, good will toward men" must be the watchword of Christianity.

Jesus said: "I thank Thee, O Father, Lord of heaven and earth, that Thou hast hid these things from the wise and prudent, and hast revealed them unto babes."

St. Paul said that without charity we are "as sounding brass, or a tinkling cymbal;" and he added: "Charity suffereth long, and is kind; ... doth not behave itself unseemly, ... thinketh no evil, ... but rejoiceth in the truth."

To hinder the unfolding truth, to ostracize whatever uplifts mankind, is of course out of the question. Such an attempt indicates weakness, fear, or malice; and such efforts arise from a spiritual lack, felt, though unacknowledged.

Let it not be heard in Boston that woman, "last at the cross and first at the sepulchre," has no rights which man is bound to respect. In natural law and in religion the right of woman to fill the highest measure of enlightened understanding and the highest places in government, is inalienable, and these rights are ably vindicated by the noblest of both sexes. This is woman's hour, with all its sweet amenities and its moral and religious reforms.

Drifting into intellectual wrestlings, we should agree to disagree; and this harmony would anchor the Church in more spiritual latitudes, and so fulfil her destiny.

Let the Word have free course and be glorified. The people clamor to leave cradle and swaddling-clothes. The spiritual status is urging its highest demands on mortals, and material history is drawing to a close. Truth cannot be stereotyped; it unfoldeth forever. "One on God's side is a majority;" and "Lo, I am with you alway," is the pledge of the Master.

The question now at issue is: Shall we have a practical, spiritual Christianity, with its healing power, or shall we have material medicine and superficial religion? The advancing hope of the race, craving health and holiness, halts for a reply; and the reappearing Christ, whose life-giving understanding Christian Science imparts, must answer the constant inquiry: "Art thou he that should come?" Woman should not be ordered to the rear, or laid on the rack, for joining the overture of angels. Theologians descant pleasantly upon free moral agency; but they should begin by admitting individual rights.

The author's ancestors were among the first settlers of New Hampshire. They reared there the Puritan standard of undefiled religion. As dutiful descendants of Puritans, let us lift their standard higher, rejoicing, as Paul did, that we are *free born*.

Man has a noble destiny; and the full-orbed significance of this destiny has dawned on the sick-bound and sin-enslaved. For the unfolding of this upward tendency to health, greatness, and goodness, I shall continue to labor and wait.

PULPIT AND PRESS.
Sixth Edition.

BY

REVEREND MARY BAKER EDDY,
DISCOVERER AND FOUNDER OF CHRISTIAN SCIENCE.
1897.

CONTENTS

PREFACE.

This volume contains scintillations from press and pulpit—utterances which epitomize the story of the birth of Christian Science, in 1866, and its progress during the ensuing thirty years. Three quarters of a century hence, when the children of to-day are the elders of the twentieth century, it will be interesting to have not only a record of the inclination given their own thoughts in the latter half of the nineteenth century, but also a registry of the rise of the mercury in the glass of the world's opinion.

It will then be instructive to turn backward the telescope of that advanced age, with its lenses of more spiritual mentality, indicating the gain of intellectual momentum, on the early footsteps of Christian Science as planted in the pathway of this generation; to note the impetus thereby given to Christianity; to con the facts surrounding the cradle of this grand verity—that the sick are healed and sinners saved, not by matter, but by Mind; and to further scan the features of the vast problem of eternal life, as expressed in the absolute power of Truth, and the actual bliss of man's existence in Science.

MARY BAKER EDDY.

February, 1895.

TO

The dear two thousand and six hundred Children,

WHOSE CONTRIBUTIONS

Of $4,460 were devoted to the Mother's Room in The First Church of Christ, Scientist, Boston,

THIS UNIQUE BOOK IS TENDERLY DEDICATED BY

MARY BAKER EDDY.

DEDICATORY SERMON.

BY REV. MARY BAKER EDDY,

First pastor of The First Church of Christ, Scientist, Boston, Mass., Delivered Jan. 6, 1895.

TEXT—Psalms xxxvi, 8. "They shall be abundantly satisfied with the fatness of thy house; and thou shalt make them drink of the river of thy pleasures."

A new year is a nursling, a babe of time, a prophecy and promise clad in white raiment, kissed—and encumbered with greetings—redolent with grief and gratitude.

An old year is time's adult, and 1893 was a distinguished character, notable for good and evil. Time past and time present, both, may pain us, but time IMPROVED is eloquent in God's praise. For due refreshment garner the memory of 1894; for if wiser by reason of its large lessons, and records deeply engraven, great is the value thereof.

Pass on returnless year!
The path behind thee is with glory crowned;
This spot whereon thou troddest was holy ground;
    Pass proudly to thy bier!

To-day being with you in spirit, what need that I should be present *in propria persona?* Were I present, methinks I should be much like the Queen of Sheba, when she saw the house Solomon had erected. In the expressive language of Holy Writ, "there was no more spirit in her;" and she said: "Behold, the half was not told me; thy wisdom and prosperity exceedeth the fame which I heard." Both without and within, the spirit of beauty dominates the Mother Church, from its mosaic flooring to the soft shimmer of its starlit dome.

Nevertheless, there is a thought higher and deeper than the edifice. Material light and shade are temporal, not eternal. Turning the attention from sublunary views, however enchanting, think for a moment with me of the house wherewith "they shall be abundantly satisfied," "Even the house not made with hands, eternal in the heavens." With the mind's eye glance at the direful scenes of the war between China and Japan. Imagine yourselves in a poorly barricaded fort, fiercely besieged by the enemy. Would you rush forth single-handed to combat the foe? Nay, would you not rather strengthen your citadel by every means in your power, and remain within the walls for its defense? Likewise should we do as metaphysicians and Christian Scientists. The real house in which "we live, move, and have our being" is Spirit, God, the eternal harmony of infinite Soul. The enemy we confront would overthrow this sublime fortress, and it behooves us to defend our heritage.

How can we do this christianly scientific work? By intrenching ourselves in the knowledge that our true temple is no human fabrication, but the superstructure of Truth, reared on the foundation of Love, and pinnacled in

Life. Such being its nature, how can our godly temple possibly be demolished, or even disturbed? Can eternity end? Can Life die? Can Truth be uncertain? Can Love be less than boundless? Referring to this temple our Master said: "Destroy this temple and in three days I will raise it up." He also said: "The kingdom of God is already within you." Know then that you possess sovereign power to think and act rightly,—and that nothing can dispossess you of this heritage and trespass on Love. If you maintain this position, who or what can cause you to sin or suffer? Our surety is in our confidence that we are indeed dwellers in Truth and Love, man's eternal mansion. Such a heavenly assurance ends all warfare, and bids tumult cease, for the good fight we have waged is over, and divine Love gives us the true sense of victory. "They shall be abundantly satisfied with the fatness of thy house; and thou shalt make them drink of the river of thy pleasures." No longer are we of the church militant, but of the church triumphant; and with Job of old we exclaim: "Yet in my flesh shall I see God." The river of his pleasures is a tributary of divine love, whose living waters have their source in God, and flow into everlasting Life. We drink of this river when all human desires are quenched, satisfied with what is pleasing to the divine Mind.

Perchance some one of you may say, "The evidence of spiritual verity in me is so small that I am afraid. I feel so far from victory over the flesh that to reach out for a present realization of my hope savors of temerity. Because of my own unfitness for such a spiritual animus my strength is naught, and my faith fails." O thou "weak and infirm of purpose." Jesus said, "Be not afraid."

"What if the little rain should say,
 'So small a drop as I
Can ne'er refresh a drooping earth,
 I'll tarry in the sky.'"

Is not a man metaphysically and mathematically number one, a unit, and therefore whole number, governed and protected by his divine Principle, God? You have simply to preserve a scientific, positive sense of unity with your divine Source and daily demonstrate this. Then you will find that one is as important a factor as duodecillions in being and doing right, and thus demonstrating deific Principle. A dewdrop reflects the sun. Each of Christ's little ones reflects the infinite One, and therefore is the seer's declaration true, that "one with God is a majority."

A single drop of water may help to hide the stars, or crown the tree with blossoms.

Who lives in Good, lives also in God,—lives in all Life, through all space. His is an individual kingdom, his diadem a crown of crowns. His existence is deathless, forever unfolding its eternal Principle. Wait patiently on illimitable Love, the lord and giver of Life. *Reflect this Life,* and with it cometh the full power of Being. "They shall be abundantly satisfied with the fatness of thy house."

In 1893 the World's Parliament of Religions, held in Chicago, used, in all its public sessions, my form of prayer since 1866; and one of the very clergymen who had publicly proclaimed me "the prayerless Mrs. Eddy," offered his audible adoration in the words I use, besides listening to an address on Christian Science from my pen, read by Judge S.J. Hanna, in that unique assembly.

When the light of one friendship after another passes from earth to heaven, we kindle in place thereof the glow of some deathless reality. Memory, faithful to goodness, holds in her secret chambers those characters of holiest sort, bravest to endure, firmest to suffer, soonest to renounce. Such was the founder of the Concord School of Philosophy—the late A. Bronson Alcott.

After the publication of SCIENCE AND HEALTH WITH KEY TO THE SCRIPTURES, his athletic mind, scholarly and serene, was the first to bedew my hope with a drop of humanity. When the press and pulpit cannonaded this book, he introduced himself to its author by saying—"I have come to comfort you." Then eloquently paraphrasing it and prophesying its prosperity, his conversation with a beauty all its own reassured me. *That prophecy is fulfilled.*

This book, in 1895, is in its ninety-first edition of one thousand copies. It is in the public libraries of the principal cities, colleges, and Universities of America; also the same in Great Britain, France, Germany, Russia, Italy, Greece, Japan, India, and China, in the Oxford University and the Victoria Institute, England; in the Academy of Greece, and the Vatican at Rome.

This book is the leaven fermenting religion; it is palpably working in the sermons, Sunday schools, and literature of our and other lands. This spiritual chemicalization is the upheaval produced when Truth is neutralizing error, and impurities are passing off. And it will continue till the antithesis of Christianity engendering the limited forms of a national or tyrannical religion yields to the church established by the Nazarene prophet and maintained on the spiritual foundation of Christ's healing.

Good, the Anglo-Saxon term for God, unites Science to Christianity. It presents to the understanding, not matter, but Mind; not the deified drug, but the goodness of God—healing and saving mankind.

The author of "Marriage of the Lamb," who made the mistake of thinking she caught her notions from my book, wrote to me in 1894, "Six months ago your book, SCIENCE AND HEALTH, was put into my hands. I had not read three pages before I realized I had found that for which I had hungered since girlhood, and was healed instantaneously of an ailment of seven years standing. I cast from me the false remedy I had vainly used and turned to the Great Physician. I went with my husband, a missionary to China, in 1884. He went out under the auspices of the Methodist Episcopal church. I feel the truth is leading us to return to Japan."

Another brilliant enunciator, seeker, and servant of Truth, the Rev. William R. Alger of Boston, signalled me kindly as my lone bark rose and fell and rode the rough sea. At a conversazione in Boston, he said, "You may find in Mrs. Eddy's metaphysical teachings, more than is dreamt of in your philosophy."

Also that renowned apostle of anti-slavery, Wendell Phillips, the native course of whose mind never swerved from the chariot-paths of justice, speaking of my work, said: "Had I young blood in my veins I would help that woman."

I love Boston, and especially the laws of the state whereof this city is the capital. To-day, as of yore, her laws have befriended progress.

Yet when I recall the past,—how the gospel of healing was simultaneously praised and persecuted in Boston,—and remember also that God is just, I wonder whether, were our dear Master in our New England metropolis at this hour, he would not weep over it, as he wept over Jerusalem! Oh, ye tears! Not in vain did ye flow. Those sacred drops were but enshrined for future use, and God has now unsealed their receptacle with His outstretched arm. Those crystal globes made morals for mankind. They will rise with joy, and with power to wash away, in floods of forgiveness, every crime, even when mistakenly committed in the name of religion.

An unjust, unmerciful, and oppressive priesthood must perish, for false prophets in the present as in the past stumble onward to their doom; while their tabernacles crumble with dry rot. "God is not mocked," and "the word of our God abideth forever."

I have ordained the Bible and the Christian Science text-book, SCIENCE AND HEALTH WITH KEY TO THE SCRIPTURES, as pastor of The First Church of Christ, Scientist, in Boston,—so long as this church is satisfied with this pastor. This is my first ordination. "They shall be abundantly satisfied with the fatness of thy house; and thou shalt make them drink of the river of thy pleasures."

All praise to the press of America's Athens,—and throughout our land, the press has spoken out historically, impartially. Like the winds telling tales through the leaves of an ancient oak, unfallen, may our church chimes repeat my thanks to the press.

Notwithstanding the perplexed condition of our nation's finances, the want and woe, with millions of dollars unemployed in our money centres, the Christian Scientists, within fourteen months, responded to the call for this church with $191,012. Not a mortgage was given nor a loan solicited, and the donors all touchingly told their privileged joy at helping to build the Mother Church. There was no urging, begging, or borrowing, only the need made known and forth came the money, or diamonds, which served to erect this "miracle in stone."

Even the children vied with their parents to meet the demand. Little hands never before devoted to menial services, shoveled snow, and babes gave kisses to earn a few pence toward this consummation. Some of these lambs my prayers had christened, but Christ will rechristen them with his own new name. "Out of the mouths of babes and sucklings hast Thou perfected praise." The resident youthful workers were called BUSY BEES.

Sweet society, precious children, your loving hearts and deft fingers distilled the nectar, and painted the finest flowers in the fabric of this history—even its centre-piece—Mother's Room in The First Church of Christ, Scientist, in

Boston. The children are destined to witness results which will eclipse oriental dreams. They belong to the twentieth century. By juvenile aid, into the building fund have come $4,460. Ah, children, you are the bulwarks of freedom, the cement of society, the hope of our race!

Brothers of the Christian Science Board of Directors, when your tireless tasks are done—well done—no Delphian lyre could break the full chords of such a rest. May the altar you have built never be shattered in our hearts, but justice, mercy, and love kindle perpetually its fires.

It was well that the brother whose appliances warm this house, warmed also our perishless hope, and nerved its grand fulfilment. Woman, true to her instinct, came to the rescue as sunshine from the clouds; so, when man quibbled over an architectural exigency, a woman climbed with feet and hands to the top of the tower, and helped settle the subject.

After the loss of our late lamented pastor, Rev. D.A. Easton, the church services were maintained by excellent sermons from the editor of the *Christian Science Journal* (who, with his better half, is a very whole man), together with the Sunday school giving this flock "drink from the river of His pleasures." Oh, glorious hope, and blessed assurance, "it is the Father's good pleasure to give you the Kingdom." Christians rejoice in secret, they have a bounty hidden from the world. Self-forgetfulness, purity, and love are treasures untold—constant prayers, prophecies, and anointings. Practice, not profession,—goodness, not doctrines,—spiritual understanding, not mere belief, gain the ear and right hand of Omnipotence, and call down blessings infinite. Faith without works is dead. The foundation of enlightened faith is Christ's teachings and *practice*. It was our Master's self-immolation, his life-giving love, healing both mind and body, that raised the deadened conscience, paralyzed by inactive faith, to a quickened sense of mortal's necessities,—and God's power and purpose to supply them. It was, in the words of the Psalmist, He "who forgiveth all thine iniquities; who healeth all thy diseases."

Rome's fallen fanes and silent Aventine is glory's tomb; her pomp and power lie low in dust. Our land, more favored, had its Pilgrim Fathers. On shores of solitude at Plymouth Rock, they planted a nation's heart,—the rights of conscience, imperishable glory. No dream of avarice or ambition broke their exalted purpose, theirs was the wish to reign in hope's reality—the realm of Love.

Christian Scientists, you have planted your standard on the Rock of Christ, the true, the spiritual idea,—the chief corner-stone in the house of our God. And our Master said: "The stone which the builders rejected the same is become the head of the corner." If you are less appreciated to-day than your forefathers, wait—for if you are as devout as they and more scientific, as progress certainly demands, your plant is immortal. Let us rejoice that chill vicissitudes have not withheld the timely shelter of this house, which descended like day spring from on high.

Divine Presence, breathe Thou thy blessing on every heart in this house. Speak out, oh, soul! This is the new-born of Spirit, this is His redeemed, this,

His beloved. May the Kingdom of God within you—with you alway—re-ascending, bear you outward, upward, Heavenward. May the sweet song of silver-throated singers, making melody more real, and the organ's voice as the sound of many waters, and the Word spoken in this sacred Temple dedicated to the ever-present God—mingle with the joy of angels and rehearse your heart's holy intents. May all whose means, energies, and prayers helped erect the Mother Church, find within it home, and *Heaven*.

CHRISTIAN SCIENCE TEXT-BOOK.

The following selections from SCIENCE AND HEALTH WITH KEY TO THE SCRIPTURES, pages 560-563, were read from the platform. The impressive stillness of the audience indicated close attention.

Revelation xii, 10-12. And I heard a loud voice saying in Heaven: Now is come salvation, and strength, and the Kingdom of our God, and the power of his Christ; for the accuser of our brethren is cast down, which accused them before our God day and night. And they overcame him by the blood of the Lamb, and by the word of their testimony; and they loved not their lives unto the death. Therefore rejoice, ye heavens, and ye that dwell in them. Woe to the inhabiters of the earth and of the sea! for the Devil is come down unto you, having great wrath, because he knoweth that he hath but a short time.

For victory over a single sin we give thanks, and magnify the Lord of Hosts. Then what shall we say of the mighty conquest over all sin? A louder song, sweeter than has ever before reached high Heaven, now rises clearer and nearer to the great heart of Christ; for the accuser is not there, and Love sends forth her primal and everlasting strain. Self-abnegation—by which we lay down all for Christ, Truth, in our warfare against error—is a rule in Christian Science. This rule clearly interprets God as divine Principle,—as Life, represented by the Father; as Truth, represented by the Son; as Love, represented by the mother. Every mortal, at some period, here or hereafter, must grapple with and overcome the mortal belief in a power opposed to God.

The Scripture, "Thou hast been faithful over a few things; I will make thee ruler over many," is literally fulfilled, when we are conscious of the supremacy of Truth, whereby the nothingness of error is seen, and we know that its nothingness is in proportion to its wickedness. He that touches the hem of Christ's robe, and masters his mortal belief, animality and hate, rejoices in the proof of healing,—in a sweet and certain sense that God is Love. Alas for those who break faith with Divine Science, and fail to strangle the serpent of sin, as well as of sickness! They are dwellers still in the deep darkness of belief. They are in the surging sea of error, not struggling to lift their heads above the drowning wave.

What must the end be? They must eventually expiate their sin through suffering. The sin which one has made his bosom companion, comes back to him at last with accelerated force; for the evil knoweth its time is short. Here the Scriptures declare that evil is temporal, not eternal. The dragon is at last stung to death by his own malice; but how many periods of self-torture it may take to remove all sin and its effects, must depend upon its obduracy.

Revelation xii, 13. And when the dragon saw
that he was cast unto the earth, he persecuted the
woman which brought forth the man child.

The march of mind and honest investigation will bring the hour when the people will chain, with fetters of some sort, the growing occultism of this period. The present apathy as to the tendency of certain active yet unseen mental agencies will finally be shocked into another extreme mortal mood,—into human indignation; for one extreme follows another.

Revelation xii, 15, 16. And the serpent
cast out of his mouth water as a flood after the
woman, that he might cause her to be carried away
of the flood. And the earth helped the woman; and
the earth opened her mouth, and swallowed up the
flood which the dragon cast out of his mouth.

Millions of unprejudiced minds—simple seekers for Truth, weary wanderers, athirst in the desert—are waiting and watching for rest and drink. Give them a cup of cold water in Christ's name, and never fear the consequences. What if the old dragon sends forth a new flood, to drown the Christ-idea? He can neither drown your voice with its roar, nor again sink the world into the deep waters of chaos and old night. In this age the earth will help the woman; the spiritual idea will be understood. Those ready for the blessing you impart will give thanks. The waters will be pacified, and Christ will command the wave.

When God heals the sick or the sinful, they should know the great benefit Mind has wrought. They should also know the great delusion of mortal mind, when it makes them sick or sinful. Many are willing to open the eyes of the people to the power of good resident in divine Mind; but they are not as willing to point out the evil in human thought, and expose its hidden mental ways of accomplishing iniquity.

Why this backwardness, since exposure is necessary, to ensure the avoidance of the evil? Because people like you better when you tell them their virtues, than when you tell them their vices. It requires the spirit of our great Master to tell a man his faults, and so risk human displeasure, for the sake of doing right and benefiting our race. Who is telling mankind of their foe in ambush? Is the informer one who sees the foe? If so, listen and be wise. Escape from evil, and designate those as unfaithful stewards, who have seen the danger and yet have given no warning.

At all times, and under all circumstances, overcome evil with Good. Know thyself, and God will supply the wisdom and the occasion for a victory over evil. Clad in the panoply of Love, human hatred cannot reach you. The cement of a higher humanity will unite all interests in the one Divinity.

HYMNS.

BY REV. MARY BAKER EDDY.
(Set to the Church chimes and sung on this occasion.)
LAYING THE CORNER STONE.

Laus Deo, it is done.
Rolled away from loving heart
Is a stone,—
Joyous, risen, we depart
Having one.

Laus Deo,—on this rock
(Heaven chiseled squarely good)
Stands His Church—
God is Love and understood
By His flock.

Laus Deo, night starlit
Slumbers not in God's embrace;
Then oh, man!
Like this stone be in thy place;
Stand, not sit.

Cold, silent, stately stone,
Dirge and song and shoutings low,
In thy heart
Dwell serene,—and sorrow? No,
It has none,
Laus Deo!

FEED MY SHEEP.

Shepherd, show me how to go
O'er the hillside steep,
How to gather, how to sow,
How to feed Thy sheep;
I will listen for Thy voice,
Lest my footsteps stray,
I will follow and rejoice
All the rugged way.

Thou wilt bind the stubborn will,
Wound the callous breast,
Make self righteousness be still,

Break earth's stupid rest;
Strangers on a barren shore
Lab'ring long and lone—
We would enter by the door,
And Thou know'st Thine own.

So when day grows dark and cold,
Tear or triumph harms,
Lead Thy lambkins to the fold,
Take them in Thine arms;
Feed the hungry, heal the heart,
Till the morning's beam;
White as wool, ere they depart—
Shepherd, wash them clean.

CHRIST MY REFUGE.

O'er waiting harpstrings of the mind
  There sweeps a strain,
Low, sad, and sweet, whose measures bind
  The power of pain

And wake a white-winged angel throng
  Of thoughts, illumed
By faith, and breathed in raptured song,
  With love perfumed.

Then His unveiled, sweet mercies show
  Life's burdens light.
We kiss the cross, and wait to know
  A world more bright.

And o'er earth's troubled, angry sea
  We see Christ walk,
And come to us, and tenderly,
  Divinely talk.

Thus Truth engrounds me on the Rock
  Upon Life's shore;
'Gainst which the winds and waves can shock,
  Oh, nevermore!

From tired joy and grief afar,
  And nearer Thee,—
Father, where Thine own children are,
  I love to be.

My prayer, some daily good to do
  To Thine, for Thee,—
Some offering pure of Love, whereto
  God leadeth me.

NOTE.—The land whereon stands The First Church of Christ, Scientist, in Boston, was first purchased by the church and society. Owing to a heavy loss they were unable to pay the mortgage, therefore I paid it and through trustees gave back the land to the church.

In 1892 I had to recover the land from the trustees, reorganize the church, and reobtain its charter—not, however, through the state commissioner, who refused to grant it, but by means of a statute of the state, and through Directors regive the land to the church. In 1895 I reconstructed my original system of ministry and church government. Thus committed to the providence of God, the prosperity of this church is unsurpassed.

From first to last the Mother church seemed type and shadow of the warfare between the flesh and Spirit, even that shadow, whose substance is the divine Spirit, imperatively propelling the greatest moral, physical, civil, and religious reform ever known on earth. In the words of the Prophet: "The shadow of a great Rock in a weary land."

This church was dedicated on January 6, anciently one of the many dates selected and observed in the East as the day of the birth and baptism of our Master Metaphysician, Jesus of Nazareth.

Christian Scientists, their children, and grandchildren to the latest generations, inevitably love one another with that love wherewith Christ loveth us. A love unselfish, unambitious, impartial, universal,—that loves only because it *is* Love. Moreover, they love their enemies, even those that hate them. This we all must do to be Christian Scientists in spirit and in truth. I long, and live, to see this love demonstrated. I am seeking and praying for it to inhabit my own heart and to be made manifest in my life. Who will unite with me in this pure purpose, and faithfully struggle till it be accomplished? Let this be our Christian endeavor society which Christ organizes and blesses.

While we entertain due respect and fellowship for what is good and doing good in all denominations of religion, and shun whatever would isolate us from a true sense of goodness in others—we cannot serve mammon.

Christian Scientists are really united to only that which is Christlike, but they are not indifferent to the welfare of any one. To perpetuate a cold distance between our denomination and other sects, and close the door on church or individuals—however much this is done to us—is not Christian Science. Go not into the way of the unchristly, but wheresoever you recognize a clear expression of God's likeness, there abide in confidence and hope.

Our unity with churches of other denominations must rest on the spirit of Christ calling us together. It cannot come from any other source. Popularity, self aggrandizement, aught that can darken in any degree our spirituality, must be set aside. Only what feeds and fills the sentiment with unworldliness, can give peace and good will towards men.

All Christian churches have one bond of unity, one nucleus or point of convergence, one prayer,—The Lord's Prayer. It is matter for rejoicing that we unite in love, and in this sacred petition with every praying assembly on earth,— "Thy kingdom come. Thy will be done on earth as in Heaven."

If the lives of Christian Scientists attest their fidelity to Truth, I predict that in the twentieth century, every Christian church in our land, and a few in far-off lands, will approximate the understanding of Christian Science sufficiently to heal the sick in His name. Christ will give to Christianity His new name, and Christendom will be classified as Christian Scientists.

When the doctrinal barriers between the churches are broken, and the bonds of peace are cemented by spiritual understanding and Love, there will be unity of spirit, and the healing power of Christ will prevail. Then shall Zion have put on her most beautiful garments, and her waste places budded and blossomed as the rose.

CLIPPINGS FROM NEWSPAPERS.

(*Daily Inter-Ocean*, Chicago, December 31, 1894.)

MARY BAKER EDDY.

Completion of The First Church of Christ, Scientist, Boston.—"Our Prayer in Stone."—Description of the Most Unique Structure in Any City.—A Beautiful Temple and Its Furnishings—Mrs. Eddy's Work and Her Influence.

BOSTON, MASS., December 28.—*Special Correspondence.*—The "great awakening" of the time of Jonathan Edwards has been paralleled daring the last decade by a wave of idealism that has swept over the country, manifesting itself under several different aspects and under various names, but each having the common identity of spiritual demand. This movement, under the guise of Christian Science, and ingenuously calling out a closer inquiry into oriental philosophy, prefigures itself to us as one of the most potent factors in the social evolution of the last quarter of the nineteenth century. History shows the curious fact that the closing years of every century are years of more intense life manifested in unrest, or in aspiration, and scholars of special research, like Professor Max Muller, assert that the end of a cycle, as is the latter part of the present century, is marked by peculiar intimations of man's immortal life.

The completion of the first Christian Science church erected in Boston strikes a keynote of definite attention. This church is in the fashionable Back Bay between Commonwealth and Huntington avenues. It is one of the most beautiful, and is certainly the most unique structure in any city. The First Church of Christ, Scientist, as it is officially called, is termed by its founders "our prayer in stone." It is located at the intersection of Norway and Falmouth streets on a plot of triangular ground, the design a Romanesque tower with a circular front and an octagonal form accented by stone porticos and turreted corners. On the front is a marble tablet with the following inscription carved in bold relief:

The First Church of Christ, Scientist, erected
Anno Domini, 1894. A testimonial to our beloved
teacher, the Rev. Mary Baker Eddy, Discoverer and
Founder of Christian Science; author of "Science
And Health, with Key to the Scriptures;" President
of the Massachusetts Metaphysical College, and the
first Pastor of this denomination.

THE CHURCH EDIFICE.

The church is built of Concord granite in light gray, with trimmings of the pink granite of New Hampshire, Mrs. Eddy's native State. The architecture is Romanesque throughout. The tower is 120 feet in height and 21-1/2 feet square. The entrances are of marble, with doors of antique oak richly carved. The windows of stained glass are very rich in pictorial effect. The lighting and cooling of the church—for cooling is a recognized feature as well as heating—are done by electricity, and the heat generated by two large boilers in the basement is distributed by the four systems with motor electric power. The partitions are of iron; the floors of marble in mosaic work, and the edifice is therefore as literally fireproof as is conceivable. The principal features are the auditorium, seating 1,100 people and capable of holding 1,500; the "Mother's room," designed for the exclusive use of Mrs. Eddy; the "directors' room," and the vestry. The girders are all of iron, the roof is of terra cotta tiles, the galleries are in plaster relief, the window frames are of iron, coated with plaster; the staircases are of iron, with marble stairs of rose pink and marble approaches.

The vestibule is a fitting entrance to this magnificent temple. In the ceiling is a sunburst with a seven-pointed star, which illuminates it. From this are the entrances leading to the auditorium, the "Mother's room," and the directors' room.

The auditorium is seated with pews of curly birch, upholstered in old rose plush. The floor is in white Italian mosaic, with frieze of the old rose, and the wainscoting repeats the same tints. The base and cap are of pink Tennessee marble. On the walls are bracketed oxidized silver lamps of Roman design, and there are frequent illuminated texts from the Bible and from Mrs. Eddy's SCIENCE AND HEALTH WITH KEY TO THE SCRIPTURES impaneled. A sunburst in the centre of the ceiling takes the place of chandeliers. There is a disc of cut glass in decorative designs covering 144 electric lights in the form of a star, which is twenty-one inches from point to point, the centre being of pure white light, and each ray under prisms which reflect the rainbow tints. The galleries are richly paneled in relief work. The organ and choir gallery is spacious and rich beyond the power of words to depict. The platform—corresponding to the chancel of an Episcopal church—is a mosaic work, with richly carved seats following the sweep of its curve, with a lamp stand of the rennaissance period on either end, bearing six richly wrought oxidized silver lamps, eight feet in height. The great organ comes from Detroit. It is one of vast compass, with æolian attachment, and cost $11,000. It is the gift of a single individual—a votive offering of gratitude for the healing of the wife of the donor.

The chime of bells includes fifteen, of fine range and perfect tone.

THE "MOTHER'S ROOM."

The "Mother's room" is approached by an entrance of Italian marble, and over the door in large golden letters on a marble tablet, is the word "Love." In this room the mosaic marble floor of white has a Romanesque border and is decorated with sprays of fig leaves bearing fruit. The room is toned in pale green with relief in old rose. The mantel is of onyx and gold. Before the great bay window hangs an Athenian lamp over two hundred years old, which will be kept always burning day and night. Leading off the "Mother's room" are toilet apartments, with full length French mirrors and every convenience.

The directors' room is very beautiful in marble approaches and rich carving, and off this is a vault for the safe preservation of papers.

The vestry seats 800 people, and opening from it are three large class rooms and the pastor's study.

The windows are a remarkable feature of this temple. There are no "memorial" windows: the entire church is a Testimonial, not a memorial—a point that the members strongly insist upon.

In the auditorium are two rose windows—one representing the heavenly city which "cometh down from God out of Heaven," with six small windows beneath, emblematic of the six water pots referred to in John xi:6. The other rose window represents the raising of the daughter of Jairus. Beneath are two small windows bearing palms of victory and others with lamps typical of Science and Health.

Another great window tells its pictorial story of the four Marys—the mother of Jesus, Mary anointing the head of Jesus, Mary washing the feet of Jesus, Mary at the resurrection; and the woman spoken of in the Apocalypse, chapter 12, God-crowned.

One more window in the auditorium represents the raising of Lazarus.

In the gallery are windows representing John on the Isle of Patmos and others of pictorial significance. In the "Mother's room" the windows are of still more unique interest. A large bay window composed of three separate panels is designed to be wholly typical of the work of Mrs. Eddy. The central panel represents her in solitude and meditation searching the scriptures by the light of a single candle, while the Star of Bethlehem shines down from above. Above this is a panel containing the Christian Science seal, and other panels are decorated with emblematic designs with the legends, "Heal the Sick," "Raise the Dead," "Cleanse the Lepers," and "Cast Out Demons."

The cross and the crown and the star are presented in appropriate decorative effect. The cost of this church is $221,000, exclusive of the land—a gift from Mrs. Eddy—which is valued at some $40,000.

THE ORDER OF SERVICE.

The order of service in the Christian Science Church does not differ widely from that of any other sect save that its service includes the use of Mrs. Eddy's book entitled SCIENCE AND HEALTH WITH KEY TO THE SCRIPTURES in perhaps equal measure to its use of the Bible—The reading is from the two alternately; the singing is from a compilation called the "Christian Science Hymnal," but its songs are for the most part those devotional hymns from Herbert, Faber, Robertson, Wesley, Browning, and other recognized devotional poets, with selections from Whittier and Lowell, as are found in the hymn books of the Unitarian churches. For the past year or two Judge Hanna, formerly of Chicago, has filled the office of pastor to the church in this city, which held its meetings in Chickering hall, and later in Copley hall, in the new Grundmann Studio building on Copley square. Preceding Judge Hanna were Rev. D.A. Easton and Rev. L.P. Norcross, both of whom had formerly been Congregational clergymen. The organizer and first pastor of the church here was Mrs. Eddy herself, of whose work I shall venture to speak, a little later, in this article.

Last Sunday I gave myself the pleasure of attending the service held in Copley hall. The spacious apartment was thronged with a congregation whose remarkable earnestness impressed the observer. There was no straggling of late-comers. Before the appointed hour every seat in the hall was filled and a large number of chairs pressed into service for the overflowing throng. The music was spirited, and the selections from the Bible and from SCIENCE AND HEALTH were finely read by Judge Hanna. Then came his sermon, which dealt directly with the command of Christ to "Heal the sick, raise the dead, cleanse the leper, cast out demons." In his admirable discourse, Judge Hanna said that while all these injunctions could, under certain conditions, be interpreted and fulfilled literally, the special lesson was to be taken spiritually—to cleanse the leprosy of sin, to cast out the demons of evil thought. The discourse was able, and helpful in its suggestive interpretation.

THE CHURCH MEMBERS.

Later I was told that almost the entire congregation was composed of persons who had either been themselves, or had seen members of their own families, healed by Christian Science treatment; and I was further told that once when a Boston clergyman remonstrated with Judge Hanna for enticing a separate congregation rather than offering their strength to unite with churches already established—I was told he replied that the Christian Science church did not recruit itself from other churches, but from the graveyards! The church numbers now 4,000 members, but this estimate, as I understand, is not limited to the Boston adherents, but includes those all over the country. The ceremonial of uniting is to sign a brief "confession of faith," written by Mrs. Eddy, and to unite in communion, which is not celebrated by outward symbols of bread and wine, but by uniting in silent prayer.

The "confession of faith" includes the declaration that the Scriptures are the guide to eternal life; that there is a Supreme Being, and his Son, and the Holy Ghost, and that man is made in his image. It affirms the atonement; it recognizes Jesus as the teacher and guide to salvation; the forgiveness of sin by God, and affirms the power of truth over error, and the need of living faith at the moment to realize the possibilities of the divine life. The entire membership of Christian Scientists throughout the world now exceeds 200,000 people. The church in Boston was organized by Mrs. Eddy, and the first meeting held on April 19, 1879. It opened with twenty-six members, and within fifteen years it has grown to its present impressive proportions, and has now its own magnificent church building, costing over $200,000, and entirely paid for when its consecration service on January 6 shall be celebrated. This is certainly a very remarkable retrospect.

Rev. Mary Baker Eddy, the founder of this denomination and discoverer of Christian Science, as they term her work in affirming the present application of the principles asserted by Jesus, is a most interesting personality. At the risk of colloquialism, I am tempted to "begin at the beginning" of my own knowledge of Mrs. Eddy, and take, as the point of departure, my first meeting with her and the subsequent development of some degree of familiarity with the work of her life which that meeting inaugurated for me.

MRS. EDDY.

It was during some year in the early '80's that I became aware—from that close contact with public feeling resulting from editorial work in daily journalism—that the Boston atmosphere was largely thrilled and pervaded by a new and increasing interest in the dominance of mind over matter, and that the central figure in all this agitation was Mrs. Eddy. To a note which I wrote her, begging the favor of an interview for press use, she most kindly replied, naming an evening on which she would receive me. At the hour named I rang the bell at a spacious house on Columbus avenue, and I was hardly more than seated before Mrs. Eddy entered the room. She impressed me as singularly graceful and winning in bearing and manner, and with great claim to personal beauty. Her figure was tall, slender, and as flexible in movement as that of a Delsarte disciple; her face, framed in dark hair and lighted by luminous blue eyes, had the transparency and rose-flush of tint so often seen in New England, and she was magnetic, earnest, impassioned. No photographs can do the least justice to Mrs. Eddy, as her beautiful complexion and changeful expression cannot thus be reproduced. At once one would perceive that she had the temperament to dominate, to lead, to control, not by any crude self-assertion, but a spiritual animus. Of course such a personality, with the wonderful tumult in the air that her large and enthusiastic following excited, fascinated the imagination. What had she originated? I mentally questioned this modern St. Catherine who was dominating her followers like any abbess of old. She told me the story of her life, so far as outward events may translate those inner experiences which alone are significant.

Mary Baker was the daughter of Mark and Abigail (Ambrose) Baker, and was born in Concord, N.H., somewhere in the early decade of 1820-'30. At the time I met her she must have been some sixty years of age, yet she had the coloring and the elastic bearing of a woman of thirty, and this, she told me, was due to the principles of Christian Science. On her father's side Mrs. Eddy came from Scotch and English ancestry, and Hannah Moore was a relative of her grandmother. Deacon Ambrose, her maternal grandfather, was known as a "godly man," and her mother was a religious enthusiast, a saintly and consecrated character. One of her brothers, Albert Baker, graduated at Dartmouth and achieved eminence as a lawyer.

MRS. EDDY AS A CHILD.

As a child Mary Baker saw visions and dreamed dreams. When eight years of age she began, like Jeanne d'Arc, to hear "voices," and for a year she heard her name called distinctly, and would often run to her mother questioning if she were wanted. One night the mother related to her the story of Samuel, and bade her, if she heard the voice again to reply as he did: "Speak, Lord, for thy servant heareth." The call came, but the little maid was afraid and did not reply. This caused her tears of remorse and she prayed for forgiveness, and promised to reply if the call came again. It came, and she answered as her mother had bidden her, and after that it ceased.

These experiences, of which Catholic biographies are full, and which history not unfrequently emphasizes, certainly offer food for meditation. Theodore

Parker related that when he was a lad at work in a field one day on his father's farm at Lexington, an old man with a snowy beard suddenly appeared at his side, and walked with him as he worked, giving him high counsel and serious thought. All inquiry in the neighborhood as to whence the stranger came or whither he went was fruitless; no one else had seen him, and Mr. Parker always believed, so a friend has told me, that his visitor was a spiritual form from another world. It is certainly true that many and many persons, whose life has been destined to more than ordinary achievement, have had experiences of voices or visions in their early youth.

At an early age Miss Baker was married to Colonel Glover, of Charleston, S.C., who lived only a year. She returned to her father's home—in 1844—and from that time until 1866 no special record is to be made.

In 1866, while living in Lynn, Mass., Mrs. Eddy (then Mrs. Glover) met with a severe accident and her case was pronounced hopeless by the physicians. There came a Sunday morning when her pastor came to bid her good-by before proceeding to his morning service as there was no probability that she would be alive at its close. During this time she suddenly became aware of a divine illumination and ministration. She requested those with her to withdraw, and reluctantly they did so, believing her delirious. Soon, to their bewilderment and fright, she walked into the adjoining room, "and they thought I had died, and that it was my apparition," she said.

THE PRINCIPLE OF DIVINE HEALING.

From that hour dated her conviction of the principle of divine healing, and that it is as true to-day as it was in the days when Jesus of Nazareth walked the earth. "I felt that the divine spirit had wrought a miracle," she said, in reference to this experience. "How, I could not tell, but later I found it to be in perfect scientific accord with the divine law." From 1866-'69, Mrs. Eddy withdrew from the world to meditate, to pray, to search the Scriptures.

"During this time," she said, in reply to my questions, "the Bible was my only text-book. It answered my questions as to the process by which I was restored to health; it came to me with a new meaning, and suddenly I apprehended the spiritual meaning of the teaching of Jesus and the principle and the law involved in spiritual science and metaphysical healing—in a word—Christian science."

Mrs. Eddy came to perceive that Christ's healing was not miraculous, but was simply a natural fulfilment of divine law—a law as operative in the world to-day as it was nineteen hundred years ago. "Divine science is begotten of spirituality," she says, "since only the 'pure in heart' can see God."

In writing of this experience, Mrs. Eddy has said:

I had learned that thought must be spiritualized
in order to apprehend Spirit. It must become
honest unselfish, and pure, in order to have the
least understanding of God in Divine Science. The
first must become last. Our reliance upon material

things must be transferred to a perception of and
dependence on spiritual things. For spirit to be
supreme in demonstration, it must be supreme in
our affections, and we must be clad with divine
power. I had learned that mind reconstructed the
body and that nothing else could. All science is a
revelation.

Through homeopathy, too, Mrs. Eddy became convinced of the principle of
mind healing, discovering that the more attenuated the drug, the more potent
was its effects.

In 1877 Mrs. Glover married Dr. Asa Gilbert Eddy, of Londonderry,
Vermont, a physician who had come into sympathy with her own views, and
who was the first to place "Christian Scientist," on the sign at his door. Dr. Eddy
died in 1882, a year after her founding of the "Metaphysical College" in Boston,
in which he taught.

The work in the Metaphysical College lasted nine years, and it was closed (in
1889) in the very zenith of its prosperity as Mrs. Eddy felt it essential to the
deeper foundation of her religious work to retire from active contact with the
world. To this college came hundreds and hundreds of students, from Europe as
well as this country. I was present at the class lectures now and then by Mrs.
Eddy's kind invitation, and such earnestness of attention as was given to her
morning talks by the men and women present I never saw equalled.

MRS. EDDY'S PERSONALITY.

On the evening that I first met Mrs. Eddy by her hospitable courtesy, I went
to her peculiarly fatigued. I came away in a state of exhilaration and energy that
made me feel I could have walked any conceivable distance. I have met Mrs.
Eddy many times since then, and always with this experience repeated.

Several years ago Mrs. Eddy removed from Columbus to Commonwealth
avenue, where, just beyond Massachusetts avenue, at the entrance to the Back
Bay Park, she bought one of the most beautiful residences in Boston. The
interior is one of the utmost taste and luxury, and the house is now occupied by
Judge and Mrs. Hanna, who are the editors of the *Christian Science Journal,* a
monthly publication, and to whose courtesy I am much indebted for some of
the data of this paper. "It is a pleasure to give any information for *The Inter-
Ocean,*" remarked Mrs. Hanna, "for it is the great daily that is so fair and so just
in its attitude toward all questions."

The increasing demands of the public on Mrs. Eddy have been, it may be,
one factor in her removal to Concord, N.H., where she has a beautiful residence,
called Pleasant View. Her health is excellent, and although her hair is white, she
retains in a great degree her energy and power; she takes a daily walk and drives
in the afternoon. She personally attends to a vast correspondence; superintends
the church in Boston, and is engaged on further writings on Christian Science.
In every sense she is the recognized head of the Christian Science Church. At
the same time it is her most earnest aim to eliminate the element of personality

from the faith. "On this point, Mrs. Eddy feels very strongly," said a gentleman to me on Christmas eve, as I sat in the beautiful drawing room, where Judge and Mrs. Hanna, Miss Elsie Lincoln, the soprano for the choir of the new church, and one or two other friends were gathered.

"Mother feels very strongly," he continued, "the danger and the misfortune of a church depending on any one personality. It is difficult not to centre too closely around a highly gifted personality."

THE FIRST ASSOCIATION.

The first Christian Scientist Association was organized on July 4, 1876, by seven persons, including Mrs. Eddy. In April, 1879, the church was founded with twenty-six members, and its charter obtained the following June. Mrs. Eddy had preached in other parishes for five years before being ordained in this church, which ceremony took place in 1881.

The first edition of Mrs. Eddy's book, SCIENCE AND HEALTH, was issued in 1875. During these succeeding twenty years it has been greatly revised and enlarged, and it is now in its ninety-first edition. It consists of fourteen chapters, whose titles are as follows: "Science, Theology, Medicine," "Physiology," "Footsteps of Truth," "Creation," "Science of Being," "Christian Science and Spiritualism," "Marriage," "Animal Magnetism," "Some Objections Answered," "Prayer," "Atonement and Eucharist," "Christian Science Practice," "Teaching Christian Science," "Recapitulation." Key to the Scriptures, Genesis, Apocalypse, and Glossary.

The Christian Scientists do not accept the belief we call spiritualism. They believe those who have passed the change of death are in so entirely different a plane of consciousness that between the embodied and disembodied there is no possibility of communication.

They are diametrically opposed to the philosophy of Karma and of reincarnation, which are the tenets of theosophy. They hold with strict fidelity to what they believe to be the literal teachings of Christ.

Yet each and all these movements, however they may differ among themselves, are phases of idealism and manifestations of a higher spirituality seeking expression.

It is good that each and all shall prosper, serving those who find in one form of belief or another their best aid and guidance, and that all meet on common ground in the great essentials of love to God and love to man as a signal proof of the divine origin of humanity which finds no rest until it finds the peace of the Lord in spirituality. They all teach that one great truth that:

God's greatness flows around our incompleteness,
Round our restlessness, his rest.
            ELIZABETH BARRETT BROWNING.

I add on the following page a little poem that I consider superbly sweet— from my friend, Miss Whiting, the talented author of "THE WORLD BEAUTIFUL."—M.B. EDDY.

AT THE WINDOW.
[*Written for the Traveller.*]

The sunset, burning low,
  Throws o'er the Charles its flood of golden light.
Dimly, as in a dream, I watch the flow
  Of waves of light.

The splendor of the sky
  Repeats its glory in the river's flow;
And sculptured angels, on the gray church tower,
  Gaze on the world below.

Dimly, as in a dream,
  I see the hurrying throng before me pass,
But 'mid them all I only see *one* face
  Under the meadow grass.

Ah, love! I only know
  How thoughts of you forever cling to me:
I wonder how the seasons come and go
  Beyond the sapphire sea?

LILLIAN WHITING.
April 15, 1888.

(*Boston Herald*, January 7, 1895.)
EXTRACT.
A TEMPLE GIVEN TO GOD.—DEDICATION OF THE MOTHER CHURCH OF CHRISTIAN SCIENCE.

Novel Method of Enabling Six Thousand Believers to Attend the Exercises—The Service Repeated Four Times—Sermon by Rev. Mary Baker Eddy, Founder of the Denomination—Beautiful Room Which the Children Built.

With simple ceremonies, four times repeated, in the presence of four different congregations, aggregating nearly 6,000 persons, the unique and costly edifice erected in Boston at Norway and Falmouth streets as a home for The First Church of Christ, Scientist, and a testimonial to the discoverer and founder of Christian Science, Rev. Mary Baker Eddy, was yesterday dedicated to the worship of God.

The structure came forth from the hands of the artisans with every stone paid for—with an appeal, not for more money, but for a cessation of the tide of contributions which continued to flow in after the full amount needed was received. From every state in the Union and from many lands, the love offerings of the disciples of Christian Science came to help erect this beautiful structure, and more than 4,000 of these contributors came to Boston from the far-off Pacific coast and the Gulf states and all the territory that lies between, to view the new-built temple and to listen to the message sent them by the teacher they revere.

From all New England the members of the denomination gathered; New York sent its hundreds, and even from the distant states came parties of 40 and 50. The large auditorium, with its capacity for holding 1,400 or 1,500 persons, was hopelessly incapable of receiving this vast throng, to say nothing of the nearly 1,000 local believers. Hence the service was repeated until all who wished had heard and seen; and each of the four vast congregations filled the church to repletion.

At 7:30 a.m. the chimes in the great stone tower, which rises 126 feet above the earth, rung out their message of "Peace on earth and good will to men."

Old familiar hymns—"All Hail the Power of Jesus's Name," and others such—were chimed until the hour for the dedication service had come.

At 9 a.m. the first congregation gathered. Before this service had closed the large vestry room and the spacious lobbies and the sidewalks around the church were all filled with a waiting multitude. At 10:30 o'clock another service began, and at noon still another. Then there was an intermission, and at 3 p.m. the service was repeated for the last time.

There was scarcely even a minor variation in the exercises at any one of these services. At 10:30 a.m., however, the scene was rendered particularly interesting by the presence of several hundred children in the central pews. These were the little contributors to the building fund, whose money was devoted to the "Mother's room," a superb apartment intended for the sole use of Mrs. Eddy. These children are known in the church as the "Busy Bees," and each of them wore a white satin badge with a golden beehive stamped upon it, and beneath the beehive the words "Mother's Room," in gilt letters.

The pulpit end of the auditorium was rich with the adornment of flowers. On the wall of the choir gallery above the platform, where the organ is to be hereafter placed, a huge seven pointed star was hung—a star of lilies resting on palms, with a centre of white immortelles, upon which in letters of red were the words: "Love-Children's Offering—1894."

In the choir and the steps of the platform were potted palms and ferns and Easter lilies. The desk was wreathed with ferns and pure white roses fastened with a broad ribbon bow. On its right was a large basket of white carnations resting on a mat of palms, and on its left a vase filled with beautiful pink roses.

Two combined choirs—that of the First Church of Christ, Scientist, of New York, and the choir of the home church, numbering thirty-five singers in all— led the singing, under the direction, respectively, of Mr. Henry Lincoln Case, and Miss Elsie Lincoln.

Judge S.J. Hanna, editor of the *Christian Science Journal*, presided over the exercises. On the platform with him were Messrs. Ira O. Knapp, Joseph Armstrong, Stephen A. Chase, and William B. Johnson, who compose the board of directors, and Mrs. Henrietta Clark Bemis, a distinguished elocutionist, and a native of Concord, New Hampshire.

The utmost simplicity marked the exercises. After an organ voluntary, the hymn, "Laus Deo, It Is Done," written by Mrs. Eddy for the corner-stone laying last spring, was sung by the congregation. Selections from the Scriptures and from SCIENCE AND HEALTH WITH KEY TO THE SCRIPTURES, were read by Judge Hanna and Dr. Eddy.

A few minutes of silent prayer came next, followed by the recitation of the Lord's prayer, with its spiritual interpretation as given in the Christian Science text-book.

The sermon prepared for the occasion by Mrs. Eddy, which was looked forward to as the chief feature of the dedication, was then read by Mrs. Bemis. Mrs. Eddy remained at her home in Concord, N.H., during the day, because, as heretofore stated in *The Herald*, it is her custom to discourage among her followers that sort of personal worship which religious teachers so often receive.

Before presenting the sermon, Mrs. Bemis read the following letter from a former pastor of the church:

> *Rev. Mary Baker Eddy*—Dear Teacher, Leader,
> Guide: Laus Deo. It is done. At last you begin to
> see the fruition of that you have worked, toiled,
> prayed for. The prayer in stone is accomplished.

Across 2,000 miles of space, as mortal sense puts
it, I send my hearty congratulations. You are
fully occupied, but I thought you would willingly
pause for an instant to receive this brief message
of congratulation. Surely it marks an era in the
blessed onward work of Christian Science. It is a
most auspicious hour in your eventful career.
While we all rejoice, yet the mother in Israel,
alone of us all, comprehends its full significance.
Yours lovingly,

LANSON P. NORCROSS.

(*Boston Sunday Globe*, January 6, 1895.)
EXTRACT.

Stately Home for Believers in Gospel Healing.—A Woman of Wealth Who Devotes All to Her Church Work.

Christian Science has shown its power over its students, as they are called, by building a church by voluntary contribution, the first of its kind, a church which will be dedicated to-day, with a quarter of a million dollars expended and free of debt.

The money has flowed in from all parts of the United States and Canada without any special appeal, and it kept coming until the custodian of funds cried "enough" and refused to accept any further checks by mail or otherwise. Men, women, and children lent a helping hand, some giving a mite and some substantial sums. Sacrifices were made in many an instance which will never be known in this world.

Christian Scientists not only say that they can effect cures of disease and erect churches, but add that they can get their buildings finished on time even when the feat seems impossible to mortal senses. Read the following from a publication of the new denomination:

One of the grandest and most helpful features of
this glorious consummation is this: that one month
before the close of the year every evidence of
material sense declared that the church's completion
within the year 1894 transcended human possibility.
The predictions of workman and onlooker alike were
that it could not be completed before April or May
of 1895.

Much was the ridicule heaped upon the hopeful, trustful ones, who declared and repeatedly asseverated to the contrary. This is indeed, then, a scientific demonstration. It has proved, in most striking manner, the oft-repeated declarations of our text-books, that the evidence of the mortal senses is unreliable.

A week ago Judge Hanna withdrew from the pastorate of the church, saying he gladly laid down his responsibilities to be succeeded by the grandest of ministers—the Bible and "SCIENCE AND HEALTH WITH KEY TO THE SCRIPTURES." This action it appears, was the result of rules made by Mrs. Eddy. The sermons hereafter will consist of passages read from the two books by readers, who will be elected each year by the congregation.

A story has been abroad that Judge Hanna was so eloquent and magnetic that he was attracting listeners who came to hear him preach rather than in search of the truth as taught. Consequently the new rules were formulated.

But at Christian Science headquarters this is denied; Mrs. Eddy says the words of the judge speak to the point, and that no such inference is to be drawn therefrom.

In Mrs. Eddy's personal reminiscences, which are published under the title of "Retrospection and Introspection," much is told of herself in detail that can only be touched upon in this brief sketch.

Aristocratic to the backbone, Mrs. Eddy takes delight in going back to the ancestral tree and in tracing those branches which are identified with good and great names both in Scotland and England.

Her family came to this country not long before the Revolution. Among the many souvenirs that Mrs. Eddy remembers as belonging to her grandparents was a heavy sword, encased in a brass scabbard, upon which had been inscribed the name of the kinsman upon whom the sword had been bestowed by Sir William Wallace of mighty Scottish fame.

Mrs. Eddy applied herself, like other girls, to her studies, though perhaps with an unusual zest, delighting in philosophy, logic, and moral science, as well as looking into the ancient languages, Hebrew, Greek, and Latin.

Her last marriage was in the spring of 1877, when, at Lynn, Mass., she became the wife of Asa Gilbert Eddy. He was the first organizer of a Christian Science Sunday-School, of which he was the superintendent, and later he attracted the attention of many clergymen of other denominations by his able lectures upon scriptural topics. He died in 1882.

Mrs. Eddy is known to her circle of pupils and admirers as the editor and publisher of the first official organ of this sect. It was called the *Journal of Christian Science*, and has had great circulation with the members of this fast-increasing faith.

In recounting her experiences as the pioneer of Christian Science, she states that she sought knowledge concerning the physical side in this research through the different schools of allopathy, homeopathy, and so forth, without receiving any real satisfaction. No ancient or modern philosophy gave her any distinct statement of the science of mind healing. She claims that no human reason has been equal to the question.

And she also defines carefully the difference in the theories between faith cure and Christian Science, dwelling particularly upon the terms belief and understanding, which are the key words respectively used in the definitions of these two healing arts.

Besides her Boston home, Mrs. Eddy has a delightful country home one mile from the state house of New Hampshire's quiet capital, an easy driving distance for her when she wishes to catch a glimpse of the world. But for the most part she lives very much retired, driving rather into the country, which is so picturesque all about Concord and its surrounding villages.

The big house, so delightfully remodeled and modernized from a primitive homestead, that nothing is left excepting the angles and pitch of the roof, is remarkably well placed upon a terrace that slopes behind the buildings, while they themselves are in the midst of green stretches of lawns, dotted with beds of flowering shrubs, with here and there a fountain or summer-house.

Mrs. Eddy took the writer straight to her beloved "lookout"—a broad piazza on the south side of the second story of the house, where she can sit in her swinging chair, revelling in the lights and shades of spring and summer greenness. Or, as just then, in the gorgeous October coloring of the whole landscape that lies below, across the farm, which stretches on through an intervale of beautiful meadows and pastures to the woods that skirt the valley of the little truant river, as it wanders eastward.

It pleased her to point out her own birthplace. Straight as the crow flies, from her piazza, does it lie on the brow of Bow hill, and then she paused and reminded the reporter that Congressman Baker from New Hampshire, her cousin, was born and bred in that same neighborhood. The photograph of Hon. Hoke Smith, another distinguished relative, adorned the mantel.

Then my eye caught her family coat of arms and the diploma given her by the Society of the Daughters of the Revolution.

The natural and lawful pride that comes with a tincture of blue and brave blood, is perhaps one of her characteristics, as is many another well born woman's. She had a long list of worthy ancestors in colonial and revolutionary days, and the McNeils, and General Knox, figure largely in her genealogy, as well as the hero who killed the ill-starred Paugus.

This big, sunny room which Mrs. Eddy calls her den—or sometimes "mother's room," when speaking of her many followers who consider her their spiritual leader—has the air of hospitality that marks its hostess herself. Mrs. Eddy has hung its walls with reproductions of some of Europe's masterpieces, a few of which had been the gifts of her loving pupils.

Looking down from the windows upon the tree-tops on the lower terrace, the reporter exclaimed: "You have lived here only four years, and yet from a barren waste of most unpromising ground has come forth all this beauty!"

"Four years!" she ejaculated; "two and a half, only two and a half years." Then, touching my sleeve and pointing, she continued: "Look at those big elms! I had them brought here in warm weather, almost as big as they are now, and not one died."

Mrs. Eddy talked earnestly of her friendships.... She told something of her domestic arrangements, of how she had long wished to get away from her busy career in Boston, and return to her native granite hills, there to build a substantial home that should do honor to that precinct of Concord.

She chose the stubbly, old farm on the road from Concord within one mile of the "Eton of America," St. Paul's school. Once bought, the will of the woman set at work, and to-day a strikingly well kept estate is the first impression given to the visitor as he approaches Pleasant View.

She employs a number of men to keep the grounds and farm in perfect order, and it was pleasing to learn that this rich woman is using her money to promote the welfare of industrious workmen in whom she takes a vital interest.

Mrs. Eddy believes that "the laborer is worthy of his hire," and, moreover, that he deserves to have a home and family of his own. Indeed, one of her motives in buying so large an estate was that she might do something for the toilers, and thus add her influence toward the advancement of better home life and citizenship.

(Boston Transcript, December 31, 1894.)

EXTRACT.

The growth of Christian Science is properly marked by the erection of a visible house of worship in this city, which will be dedicated tomorrow. It has cost $200,000, and no additional sums outside of the subscriptions are asked for. This particular phase of religious belief has impressed itself upon a large and increasing number of Christian people, who have been tempted to examine its principles, and doubtless have been comforted and strengthened by them. Any new movement will awaken some sort of interest. There are many who have worn off the novelty and are thoroughly carried away with the requirements, simple and direct as they are, of Christian Science. The opposition against it from the so-called orthodox religious bodies keeps up a while, but after a little skirmishing, finally subsides. No one religious body holds the whole of truth, and whatever is likely to show even some one side of it will gain followers and live down any attempted repression.

Christian Science does not strike all as a system of truth. If it did, it would be a prodigy. Neither does the Christian faith produce the same impressions upon all. Freedom to believe or to dissent is a great privilege in these days. So when a number of conscientious followers apply themselves to a matter like Christian Science, they are enjoying that liberty which is their inherent right as human beings, and though they cannot escape censure, yet they are to be numbered among the many pioneers who are searching after religious truth. There is really nothing settled. Every truth is more or less in a state of agitation. The many who have worked in the mine of knowledge are glad to welcome others who have different methods, and with them bring different ideas.

It is too early to predict where this movement will go, and how greatly it will affect the well established methods. That it has produced a sensation in religious circles, and called forth the implements of theological warfare, is very well known. While it has done this, it may, on the other hand, have brought a benefit. Ere this many a new project in religious belief has stirred up feeling, but as time has gone on, compromises have been welcomed.

The erection of this temple will doubtless help on the growth of its principles. Pilgrims from everywhere will go there in search of truth, and some may be satisfied and some will not. Christian Science cannot absorb the world's thought. It may get the share of attention it deserves, but it can only aspire to take its place alongside other great demonstrations of religious belief which have done something good for the sake of humanity.

Wonders will never cease. Here is a church whose treasurer has to send out word that no sums except those already subscribed can be received! The Christian Scientists have a faith of the mustard-seed variety. What a pity some of our practical Christian folk have not a faith approximate to that of these "impractical" Christian Scientists.

(*Jackson Patriot*, Jackson, Mich. January 20, 1895.)
EXTRACT.
CHRISTIAN SCIENCE.
The erection of a massive temple in Boston by Christian Scientists, at a cost of over $200,000, love offerings of the disciples of MARY BAKER EDDY, reviver of the ancient faith and author of the text-book from which, with the New Testament at the foundation, believers receive light, health, and strength, is evidence of the rapid growth of the new movement. We call it new. It is not. The name Christian Science alone is new. At the beginning of Christianity it was

taught and practiced by Jesus and his disciples. The Master was the great healer. But the wave of materialism and bigotry that swept over the world for fifteen centuries, covering it with the blackness of the Dark Ages, nearly obliterated all vital belief in his teachings. The Bible was a sealed book. Recently a revived belief in what he taught is manifest, and Christian Science is one result. No new doctrine is proclaimed, but there is the fresh development of a principle that was put into practice by the founder of Christianity nineteen hundred years ago, though practiced in other countries at any earlier date. "The thing that hath been, it is that which shall be; and that which is done, is that which shall be done, and there is no new thing under the sun."

The condition which Jesus of Nazareth, on various occasions during the three years of his ministry on earth, declared to be essential, in the mind of both healer and patient, is contained in the one word—FAITH. Can drugs suddenly cure leprosy? When the ten lepers were cleansed and one returned to give thanks in Oriental phrase, Jesus said to him: "Arise, go thy way; thy faith hath made thee whole." That was Christian Science. In his "Law of Psychic Phenomena" Hudson says: "That word, more than any other, expresses the whole law of human felicity and power in this world and of salvation in the world to come." It is that attribute of mind which elevates man above the level of the brute, and gives dominion over the physical world. It is the essential element of success in every field of human endeavor. It constitutes the power of the human soul. When Jesus of Nazareth proclaimed its potency from the hilltops of Palestine he gave to mankind the key to health and heaven, and earned the title of "Savior of the World." Whittier, grandest of mystic poets, saw the truth:

"That healing gift He lends to them
  Who use it in His name;
The power that filled his garment's hem
  Is evermore the same."

  Again, in a poem entitled "The Master," he wrote:

"The healing of his seamless dress
  Is by our beds of pain;
We touch Him in life's throng and press,
  And we are whole again."

[1] That Jesus operated in perfect harmony with natural law, not in defiance, suppression, or violation of it, we cannot doubt. The perfectly natural is the perfectly spiritual. Jesus enunciated and exemplified the principle; and,

---

[1] About 1868, the author of SCIENCE AND HEALTH healed Mr. Whittier with one visit, at his home in Amesbury, of incipient pulmonary consumption.—M.B. EDDY.]

obviously, the conditions requisite in psychic healing to-day are the same as were necessary in apostolic times. We accept the statement of Hudson: "There was no law of nature violated or transcended. On the contrary, the whole transaction was in perfect obedience to the laws of nature. He understood the law perfectly, as no one before him understood it; and in the plentitude of his power he applied it where the greatest good could be accomplished." A careful reading of the accounts of his healings, in the light of modern science, shows that he observed, in his practice of mental therapeutics, the conditions of environment and harmonious influence that are essential to success. In the case of Jairus' daughter they are fully set forth. He kept the unbelievers away, "put them all out," and permitting only the father and mother, with his closest friends and followers, Peter, James, and John, in the chamber with him, and having thus the most perfect obtainable environment, he raised the daughter to life.

"Not in blind caprice of will,
Not in cunning sleight of skill,
Not for show of power, was wrought
Nature's marvel in Thy thought."

In a previous article we have referred to cyclic changes that came during the last quarter of preceding centuries. Of our remarkable nineteenth century not the least eventful circumstance is the advent of Christian Science. That it should be the work of a woman is the natural outcome of a period notable for her emancipation from many of the thraldoms, prejudices, and oppressions of the past. We do not, therefore, regard it as a mere coincidence that the first edition of Mrs. Eddy's "SCIENCE AND HEALTH" should have been published in 1875. Since then she has revised it many times, and the ninety-first edition is announced. Her discovery was first called "the science of divine metaphysical healing." Afterward she selected the name Christian Science. It is based upon what is held to be scientific certainty, namely,—that all causation is of Mind, every effect has its origin in desire and thought. The theology—if we may use the word—of Christian Science is contained in the volume entitled "SCIENCE AND HEALTH WITH KEY TO THE SCRIPTURES."

The present Boston congregation was organized April 19, 1879, and has now over 4,000 members. It is regarded as the parent organization, all others being branches, though each is entirely independent in the management of its own affairs. Truth is the sole recognized authority. Of actual members of different congregations there are between 100,000 and 200,000. One or more organized societies have sprung up in New York, Chicago, Buffalo, Cleveland, Cincinnati, Philadelphia, Detroit, Toledo, Milwaukee, Madison, Scranton, Peoria, Atlanta, Toronto, and nearly every other centre of population, besides a large and growing number of receivers of the faith among the members of all the churches and non-church-going people. In some churches a majority of the members are Christian Scientists, and, as a rule, are the most intelligent.

Space does not admit of an elaborate presentation on the occasion of the erection of the temple, in Boston, the dedication taking place on the 6th of January, of one of the most remarkable, helpful, and powerful movements of the last quarter of the century. Christian Science has brought hope and comfort to many weary souls. It makes people better and happier. Welding Christianity and Science, hitherto divorced because dogma and truth could not unite, was a happy inspiration.

"And still we love the evil cause,
  And of the just effect complain;
We tread upon life's broken laws,
  And mourn our self-inflicted pain."

(*The Outlook*, New York, January 19, 1895.)
A CHRISTIAN SCIENCE CHURCH.
A great Christian Science Church was dedicated in Boston on Sunday, the 6th inst. It is located at Norway and Falmouth streets, and is intended to be a testimonial to the discoverer and founder of Christian Science, the Rev. Mary Baker Eddy. The building is fireproof, and cost over $200,000. It is entirely paid for, and contributions for its erection came from every state in the Union, and from many lands. The auditorium is said to seat between fourteen and fifteen hundred, and was thronged at the four services on the day of dedication. The sermon prepared by Mrs. Eddy was read by Mrs. Bemis. It rehearsed the significance of the building, and reënunciated the truths which will find emphasis there. From the description we judge that it is one of the most beautiful buildings in Boston, and, indeed, in all New England. Whatever may be thought of the peculiar tenets of the Christian Scientists, and whatever difference of opinion there may be concerning the organization of such a church, there can be no question but that the adherents of this church have proved their faith by their works.

(*American Art Journal*, New York, January 26, 1895.)
"OUR PRAYER IN STONE."
Such is the excellent name given to a new Boston church. Few people outside its own circles, realize how extensive is the belief in Christian Science. There are several sects of mental healers, but this new edifice on Back Bay, just off Huntington avenue, not far from the big Mechanics building and the proposed site of the new Music hall, belongs to the followers of Rev. Mary Baker Glover Eddy, a lady born of an old New Hampshire family, who, after many vicissitudes, found herself in Lynn, Mass., healed by the power of Divine Mind, and thereupon devoted herself to imparting this faith to her fellow beings. Coming to Boston about 1880 she began teaching, gathered an association of students, and organized a church. For several years past she has lived in Concord, N.H., near her birthplace, owning a beautiful estate called Pleasant View; but thousands of believers throughout this country have joined the

Mother Church in Boston and have now erected this edifice at a cost of over two hundred thousand dollars, every bill being paid.

Its appearance is shown in the pictures we are permitted to publish. In the belfry is a set of tubular chimes. Inside is a basement room, capable of division into seven excellent class rooms, by the use of movable partitions. The main auditorium has wide galleries, and will seat over a thousand in its exceedingly comfortable pews. Scarcely any woodwork is to be found. The floors are all mosaic, the steps marble, and the walls stone. It is rather dark, often too much so for comfortable reading, as all the windows are of colored glass, with pictures symbolic of the tenets of the organization. In the ceiling is a beautiful sunburst window. Adjoining the chancel is a pastor's study; but for an indefinite time their prime instructor has ordained that the only pastor shall be the Bible, with her book called "SCIENCE AND HEALTH WITH KEY TO THE SCRIPTURES." In the tower is a room devoted to her, and called Mother's Room, furnished with all conveniences for living, should she wish to make it a home by day or night. Therein is a portrait of her in stained glass; and an electric light, behind an antique lamp, kept perpetually burning in her honor; though she has not yet visited her temple, which was dedicated on New Year's Sunday, in a somewhat novel way.

There was no special sentence or prayer of consecration; but continuous services were held from nine to four o'clock, every hour and a half, so long as there were attendants; and some people heard these exercises four times repeated. The printed program was for some reason not followed, certain hymns and psalms being omitted. There was singing by a choir and congregation. The *pater noster* was repeated in the way peculiar to Christian Scientists, the congregation repeating one sentence and the leader responding with its parallel interpretation by Mrs. Eddy. Antiphonal paragraphs were read from the book of Revelation and her work respectively. The sermon, prepared by Mrs. Eddy, was well adapted for its purpose, and read by a professional elocutionist, not an adherent of the order, Mrs. Henrietta Clark Bemis, in a clear, emphatic style. The solo singer, however, was a Scientist, Miss Elsie Lincoln; and on the platform sat Joseph Armstrong, formerly of Kansas, and now the business manager of the publication society, with the other members of the Christian Science Board of Directors—Ira C. Knapp, Edward P. Bates, Stephen A. Chase,—gentlemen officially connected with the movement. The children of believing families collected the money for the Mother Room, and seats were especially set apart for them at the second dedicatory service. Before one service was over and the auditors left by the rear doors, the front vestibule and street (despite the snowstorm) were crowded with others, waiting admission.

On the next Sunday the new order of service went into operation. There was no address of any sort, no notices, no explanation of Bible or their text-book. Judge Hanna, who was a Colorado lawyer before coming into this work, presided, reading in clear, manly, and intelligent tones, the quarterly Bible lesson, which happened that day to be on Jesus' miracle of loaves and fishes. Each paragraph he supplemented first with illustrative Scripture parallels, as set down for him, and then by passages selected for him from Mrs. Eddy's book. The place was again crowded, many having remained over a week from among the thousands of adherents who had come to Boston for this auspicious occasion from all parts of the country. The organ, made by Farrand & Votey in Detroit, at a cost of eleven thousand dollars, is the gift of a wealthy Universalist gentleman, but was not ready for the opening. It is to fill the recess behind the spacious platform, and is described as containing pneumatic windchests throughout, and having an æolian attachment. It is of three-manual compass, C.C.C. to C.4, 61 notes; and pedal compass, C.C.C. to F.30. The great organ has double open diapason (stopped bass), open diapason, dulciana, viola di gambi, doppel flute, hohl flute, octave, octave quint, superoctave, and trumpet,—65 pipes each. The swell organ has bourdon, open diapason, salicional, æoline, stopped diapason, gemshorn, flute harmonique, flageolet, cornet—3 ranks, 183,—cornopean, oboe, vox humana—61 pipes each. The choir organ, enclosed in separate swell-box, has geigen principal, dolce, concert flute, quintadena, fugara, flute d'amour, piccolo harmonique, clarinet,—61 pipes each. The pedal organ has open diapson, bourden, lieblich gedeckt (from stop 10), violoncello-wood,—30 pipes each. Couplers: swell to great; choir to great; swell to choir; swell to great octaves, swell to great sub-octaves; choir to great sub-octaves; swell octaves; swell to pedal; great to pedal; choir to pedal. Mechanical accessories: swell tremulant, choir tremulant, bellows signal; wind indicator. Pedal movements: three affecting great and pedal stops, three affecting swell and pedal stops; great to pedal reversing pedal; crescendo and full organ pedal; balanced great and choir pedal; balanced swell pedal.

Beautiful suggestions greet you in every part of this unique church, which is practical as well as poetic, and justifies the name given by Mrs. Eddy, which stands at the head of this sketch. J.H.W.

(*Boston Journal*, January 7, 1895.)
CHIMES RANG SWEETLY.

Much admiration was expressed by all those fortunate enough to listen to the first peal of the chimes in the tower of The First Church of Christ, Scientist, corner of Falmouth and Norway streets, dedicated yesterday. The sweet, musical tones attracted quite a throng of people, who listened with delight.

The chimes were made by the United States Tubular Bell Company, of Methuen, Mass., and are something of a novelty in this country, though for some time well and favorably known in the Old Country, especially in England.

They are a substitution of tubes of drawn brass for the heavy cast bells of old-fashioned chimes. They have the advantage of great economy of space, as well as of cost, a chime of fifteen bells not occupying a space of more than five by eight feet.

Where the old-fashioned chimes required a strong man to ring them, these can be rung from an electric key board, and even when rung by hand require but little muscular power to manipulate them, and call forth all the purity and sweetness of their tones. The quality of tone is something superb, being rich and mellow. The tubes are carefully tuned, so that the harmony is perfect. They have all the beauties of a great Cathedral chime, with infinitely less expense.

There is practically no limit to the uses to which these bells may be put. They can be called into requisition in theatres, concert halls, and public buildings, as they range in all sizes, from those described down to little sets of silver bells that might be placed on a small centre table.

(*The Republic*, Washington, D.C., February 2, 1895.)
EXTRACT.
CHRISTIAN SCIENCE.

Mary Baker Eddy the "Mother" of the Idea.—She Has an Immense Following Throughout the United States, and a Church Costing $250,000 Was Recently Built in Her Honor at Boston.

"My faith has the strength to nourish trees as well as souls," was the remark Rev. Mary Baker Eddy, the "mother" of Christian Science, made recently as she pointed to a number of large elms that shade her delightful country home, in Concord, N.H. "I had them brought here in warm weather almost as big as they are now, and not one died." This is a remarkable statement, but it is made by a remarkable woman, who has originated a new phase of religious belief, and who numbers over 100,000 intelligent people among her devoted followers.

The great hold she has upon this army was demonstrated in a very tangible and material manner recently when "The First Church of Christ, Scientist," erected at a cost of $250,000, was dedicated in Boston. This handsome edifice was paid for before it was begun, by the voluntary contributions of Christian Scientists all over the country, and a tablet imbedded in its wall declares that it was built as "a testimonial to our beloved teacher, Rev. Mary Baker Eddy, discoverer and founder of Christian Science, author of its textbook, 'SCIENCE AND HEALTH WITH KEY TO THE SCRIPTURES,' president of the Massachusetts Metaphysical college and the first pastor of this denomination."

There is usually considerable difficulty in securing sufficient funds for the building of a new church, but such was not the experience of Rev. Mary Baker Eddy. Money came freely from all parts of the United States. Men, women, and children contributed, some giving a pittance, others donating large sums. When the necessary amount was raised the custodian of the funds was compelled to refuse further contributions in order to stop the continued inflow of money from enthusiastic Christian Scientists.

Mrs. Eddy says she discovered Christian Science in 1866. She studied the Scriptures and the sciences, she declares, in a search for the great curative principle. She investigated allopathy, homeopathy, and electricity, without finding a clew; and modern philosophy gave her no distinct statement of the science of mind healing. After careful study she became convinced that the curative principle was the Deity.

(*New York Tribune*, February 7, 1895.)
EXTRACT.

Boston has just dedicated the first church of the Christian Scientists in commemoration of the founder of that sect, the Rev. Mary Baker Eddy, drawing together 6,000 people to participate in the ceremonies, showing that belief in that curious creed is not confined to its original apostles and promulgators, but that it has penetrated what is called the New England mind to an unlooked-for extent, in inviting the Eastern churches and the Anglican fold to unity with Rome, the Holy Father should not overlook the Boston sect of Christian Scientists, which is rather small and new, to be sure, but is undoubtedly an interesting faith and may have a future before it, whatever attitude Rome may assume toward it.

(*Journal*, Kansas City, Mo., January 10, 1895.)
EXTRACT.
GROWTH OF A FAITH.
Attention is directed to the progress which has been made by what is called Christian Science by the dedication at Boston of "The First Church of Christ, Scientist." It is a most beautiful structure of gray granite, and its builders call it their "prayer in stone," which suggests to recollection the story of the cathedral of Amiens, whose architectural construction and arrangement of statuary and paintings made it to be called the Bible of that city. The Frankish church was reared upon the spot where, in pagan times, one bitter winter day, a Roman soldier parted his mantle with his sword and gave half of the garment to a naked beggar; and so was memorialized in art and stone what was called the divine spirit of giving, whose unbelieving exemplar afterward became a saint. The Boston church similarly expresses the faith of those who believe in what they term the divine art of healing, which, to their minds, exists as much to-day as it did when Christ healed the sick.

The first church organization of this faith was founded fifteen years ago with a membership of only twenty-six, and since then the number of believers has grown with remarkable rapidity, until now, there are societies in every part of the country. This growth, it is said, proceeds more from the graveyards than from conversions from other churches, for most of those who embrace the faith claim to have been rescued from death miraculously under the injunction to "heal the sick, raise the dead, cleanse the leper, and cast out demons." They hold with strict fidelity to what they conceive to be the literal teachings of the Bible as expressed in its poetical and highly figurative language.

Altogether the belief and service are well suited to satisfy a taste for the mystical which, along many lines, has shown an uncommon development in this country during the last decade, and which is largely Oriental in its choice. Such a rapid departure from long respected views as is marked by the dedication of this church, and others of kindred meaning, may reasonably excite wonder as to how radical is to be this encroachment upon prevailing faiths, and whether some of the pre-Christian ideas of the Asiatics are eventually to supplant those in company with which our civilization has developed.

(*Montreal Daily Herald* Saturday, February 2, 1895.)

EXTRACT.

CHRISTIAN SCIENCE.

Sketch of Its Origin and Growth—The Montreal Branch.

"If you would found a new faith, go to Boston," has been said by a great American writer. This is no idle word, but a fact borne out by circumstances. Boston can fairly claim to be the hub of the logical universe, and an accurate census of the religious faiths which are to be found there to-day, would probably show a greater number of them than even Max O'Rells famous enumeration of John Bull's creeds.

Christian Science, or the principle of divine healing, is one of those movements which seek to give expression to a higher spirituality. Founded twenty-five years ago, it was still practically unknown a decade since, but to-day it numbers over a quarter of a million of believers, the majority of whom are in the United States, and is rapidly growing. In Canada, also, there is a large number of members. Toronto and Montreal have strong churches, comparatively, while in many towns and villages single believers or little knots of them are to be found.

It was exactly 100 years from the date of the Declaration of Independence, when on July 4, 1876, the first Christian Scientist Association was organized by seven persons, of whom the foremost was Mrs. Eddy. The church was founded in April. 1879, with twenty-six members, and a charter was obtained two months later. Mrs. Eddy assumed the pastorship of the church during its early years, and in 1881 was ordained, being now known as the Rev. Mary Baker Eddy.

The Massachusetts Metaphysical College was founded by Mrs. Eddy in 1881, and here she taught the principles of the faith for nine years. Students came to it in hundreds from all parts of the world, and many are now pastors or in practice. The college was closed in 1889, as Mrs. Eddy felt it necessary for the interests of her religious work to retire from active contact with the world. She now lives in a beautiful country residence in her native state.

(*The American*, Baltimore, Md., January 14, 1895.)

EXTRACT.

MRS. EDDY'S DISCIPLES.

It is not generally known that a Christian Science congregation was organized in this city about a year ago. It now holds regular services in the parlor of the residence of the pastor, at 1414 Linden avenue. The dedication in Boston last Sunday of the Christian Science Church, called the Mother Church, which cost over $200,000, adds interest to the Baltimore organization. There are many other church edifices in the United States owned by Christian Scientists. Christian Science was founded by Mrs. Mary Baker Eddy. The Baltimore congregation was organized at a meeting held at the present location on February 27, 1894.

Dr. Hammond, the pastor, came to Baltimore about three years ago to organize this movement. Miss Cross came from Syracuse, N.Y., about eighteen months ago. Both were under the instruction of Mrs. Mary Baker Eddy, the founder of the movement.

Dr. Hammond says he was converted to Christian Science by being cured by Mrs. Eddy of a physical ailment some twelve years ago, after several doctors had pronounced his case incurable. He says they use no medicines, but rely on Mind for cure, believing that disease comes from evil and sick-producing thoughts, and that, if they can so fill the mind with good thoughts as to leave no room there for the bad, they can work a cure. He distinguishes Christian Science from the faith cure and added: "This Christian Science really is a return to the ideas of primitive Christianity. It would take a small book to explain fully all about it, but I may say that the fundamental idea is that God is Mind, and we interpret the Scriptures wholly from the spiritual or metaphysical standpoint. We find in this view of the Bible the power fully developed to heal the sick. It is not faith cure, but it is an acknowledgment of certain Christian and scientific laws, and to work a cure the practitioner must understand these laws aright. The patient may gain a better understanding than the church has had in the past. All churches have prayed for the cure of disease, but they have not done so in an intelligent manner, understanding and demonstrating the Christ-healing."

(*The Reporter*, Lebanon, Ind., January 18, 1895.)

EXTRACT.

DISCOVERED CHRISTIAN SCIENCE.

Remarkable Career of Rev. Mary Baker Eddy, Who Has Over 100,000 Followers.

Rev. Mary Baker Eddy, discoverer and founder of Christian Science, author of its textbook, "SCIENCE AND HEALTH WITH KEY TO THE SCRIPTURES," president of the Massachusetts Metaphysical college, and first pastor of the Christian Science denomination, is without doubt one of the most remarkable women in America. She has within a few years founded a sect that has over 100,000 converts, and very recently saw completed in Boston as a testimonial to her labors, a handsome fire proof church that cost $250,000, and was paid for by Christian Scientists all over the country.

Mrs. Eddy asserts that in 1866 she became certain that "all causation was mind and every effect a mental phenomenon." Taking her text from the Bible, she endeavored in vain to find the great curative principle—the Deity—in philosophy and schools of medicine, and she concluded that the way of salvation demonstrated by Jesus was the power of truth over all error, sin, sickness, and death. Thus originated the divine or spiritual science of mind healing, which she termed Christian Science. She has a palatial home in Boston and a country seat in Concord, N.H. The Christian Science church has a membership of 4,000, and 800 of the members are Bostonians.

(*N.Y. Commercial Advertiser*, January 9, 1895.)

The idea that Christian Science has declined in popularity is not borne out by the voluntary contribution of a quarter of a million dollars for a memorial church for Mrs. Eddy, the inventor of this cure. The money comes from Christian Science believers exclusively.

(*The Post*, Syracuse, New York, February 1, 1895.)

DO NOT BELIEVE SHE WAS DEIFIED.

Christian Scientists of Syracuse Surprised at the News About Mrs. Mary Baker Eddy, Founder of the Faith.

Christian Scientists in this city, and in fact all over the country, have been startled and greatly discomfited over the announcements in New York papers that Mrs. Mary Baker G. Eddy, the acknowledged Christian Science leader, has been exalted by various dignitaries of the faith....

It is well known that Mrs. Eddy has resigned herself completely to the study and foundation of the faith to which many thousands throughout the United States are now so entirely devoted. By her followers and co-believers she is unquestionably looked upon as having a divine mission to fulfill, and as though inspired in her great task by supernatural power.

For the purpose of learning the feeling of Scientists in this city toward the reported deification of Mrs. Eddy, a *Post* reporter called upon a few of the leading members of the faith yesterday and had a number of very interesting conversations upon the subject.

Mrs. D.W. Copeland of University avenue was one of the first to be seen. Mrs. Copeland is a very pleasant and agreeable lady, ready to converse, and evidently very much absorbed in the work to which she has given so much of her attention. Mrs. Copeland claims to have been healed a number of years ago by Christian Scientists, after she had practically been given up by a number of well known physicians.

"And for the past eleven years," said Mrs. Copeland, "I have not taken any medicine or drugs of any kind, and yet have been perfectly well."

In regard to Mrs. Eddy, Mrs. Copeland said that she was the founder of the faith, but that she had never claimed, nor did she believe that Mrs. Lathrop had, that Mrs. Eddy had any power other than that which came from God and through faith in Him and His teachings.

"The power of Christ has been dormant in mankind for ages," added the speaker, "and it was Mrs. Eddy's mission to revive it. In our labors we take Christ as an example, going about doing good and healing the sick. Christ has told us to do His work, naming as one great essential that we have faith in Him.

"Did you ever hear of Jesus' taking medicine Himself, or giving it to others?" inquired the speaker. "Then why should we worry ourselves about sickness and disease? If we become sick God will care for us, and will send to us those who have faith, who believe in His unlimited and divine power." Mrs. Eddy was strictly an ardent follower after God. She had faith in him, and she cured herself of a deathly disease through the mediation of her God. Then she secluded herself from the world for three years and studied and meditated over His divine word. She delved deep into the Biblical passages, and at the end of the period came from her seclusion one of the greatest Biblical scholars of the age. Her mission was then the mission of a Christian to do good and heal the sick, and this duty she faithfully performed. She of herself had no power. But God has fulfilled His promises to her and to the world. "If ye have faith ye can move mountains."

Mrs. Henrietta N. Cole is also a very prominent member of the church. When seen yesterday she emphasized herself as being of the same theory as Mrs. Copeland. Mrs. Cole has made a careful and searching study in the beliefs of Scientists and is perfectly versed in all their beliefs and doctrines. She stated that man of himself has no power, but that all comes from God. She placed no credit whatever in the reports from New York that Mrs. Eddy has been accredited as having been deified. She referred the reporter to the large volume which Mrs. Eddy had herself written, and said that no more complete and yet concise idea of her belief could be obtained than by a perusal of it.

(*New York Herald*, February 1, 1895.)
MRS. EDDY SHOCKED.
[BY TELEGRAPH TO THE HERALD.]
CONCORD, N.H., February 4, 1895.—The article published in the HERALD on January 29, regarding a statement made by Mrs. Laura Lathrop, pastor of the Christian Science congregation, that meets every Sunday in Hodgson Hall, New York, was shown to Mrs. Mary Baker Eddy, the Christian Science "discoverer," to-day.

Mrs. Eddy preferred to prepare a written answer to the interrogatory, which she did in this letter, addressed to the editor of the HERALD:

"A despatch is given me, calling for an interview to answer for myself, 'Am I the second Christ?'

"Even the question shocks me. What I am is for God to declare in his infinite mercy. As it is I claim nothing more than what I am, the discoverer and founder of Christian Science, and the blessing it has been to mankind which eternity enfolds.

"I think Mrs. Lathrop was not understood. If she said aught with intention to be thus understood, it is not what I have taught her, and not at all as I have heard her talk.

"My books and teachings maintain but one conclusion and statement of the Christ and the deification of mortals.

"Christ is individual, and one with God, in the sense of Divine Principle and its compound divine idea.

"There was, is and never can be but one God, one Christ, one Jesus of Nazareth. Whoever in any age expresses most of the spirit of Truth and Love, the Principle of God's Idea, has most of the spirit of Christ, of that Mind which was in Christ Jesus.

"If Christian Scientists find in my writings, teachings, and example a greater degree of this spirit than in others, they can justly declare it. But to think or speak of me in any manner as a Christ, is sacrilegious. Such a statement would not only be false, but the absolute antipode of Christian Science, and would savor more of heathenism, than of my doctrines.

"MARY BAKER EDDY."

(*The Globe*, Toronto, Canada, January 12, 1895.)

EXTRACT.

CHRISTIAN SCIENTISTS.

Dedication to the Founder of the Order of a Beautiful Church at Boston.— Many Toronto Scientists Present.

The Christian Scientists of Toronto to the number of thirty took part in the ceremonies at Boston last Sunday and for the day or two following, by which the members of that faith all over North America celebrated the dedication of the church constructed in the great New England capital as a Testimonial to the discoverer and founder of Christian Science, Rev. Mary Baker Eddy.

The temple is believed to be the most nearly fire-proof church structure on the continent, the only combustible material used in its construction being that used in the doors and pews. A striking feature of the church is a beautiful apartment known as the "Mother's Room," which is approached through a superb archway of Italian marble set in the wall. The furnishing of the "Mother's Room" is described as "particularly beautiful, and blends harmoniously with the pale green and gold decoration of the walls. The floor is of mosaic in elegant designs, and two alcoves are separated from the apartment by rich hangings of deep green plush, which in certain lights has a shimmer of silver. The furniture frames are of white mahogany in special designs, elaborately carved, and the upholstery is in white and gold tapestry. A superb mantel of Mexican onyx with gold decoration adorns the south wall, and before the hearth is a large rug composed entirely of skins of the eider-down duck, brought from the Arctic regions. Pictures and bric-a-brac everywhere suggest the tribute of loving friends. One of the two alcoves is a retiring room, and the other a lavatory in which the plumbing is all heavily plated with gold."

(*Evening Monitor*, Concord, N.H., February 27, 1895.)

AN ELEGANT SOUVENIR.

Rev. Mary Baker Eddy Memorialized by a Christian Science Church.

Rev. Mary Baker Eddy, discoverer of Christian Science, has received from the members of The First Church of Christ, Scientist, Boston, an invitation to formally accept the magnificent new edifice of worship which the church has just erected.

The invitation itself is one of the most chastely elegant memorials ever prepared, and is a scroll of solid gold, suitably engraved, and encased in a handsome plush casket with white silk linings. Attached to the scroll is a golden key of the church structure.

The inscription reads thus:

DEAR MOTHER: During the year eighteen hundred and ninety-four a church edifice was erected at the intersection of Falmouth and Norway streets in the city of Boston, by the loving hands of four thousand members. This edifice is built as a Testimonial to truth as revealed by divine Love through you to this age.

You are hereby most lovingly invited to visit and formally accept this Testimonial on the twentieth day of February, eighteen hundred and ninety-five at high noon.

The First Church of Christ, Scientist, at Boston, Mass.

By EDWARD P. BATES, CAROLINE S. BATES.

To the Reverend Mary Baker Eddy, Boston, January 6th, 1895.

(*People and Patriot*, Concord, N.H., February 27, 1895.)

MAGNIFICENT TESTIMONIAL.

Members of The First Church of Christ, Scientist, at Boston have forwarded to Mrs. Mary Baker Eddy of this city, the founder of Christian Science, a Testimonial which is probably one of the most magnificent examples of the goldsmith's art ever wrought in this country. It is in the form of a gold scroll, twenty-six inches long, nine inches wide, and an eighth of an inch thick.

It bears upon its face the following inscription cut in script letters:

"Dear Mother,

"During the year 1894, a church edifice was erected at the intersection of Falmouth and Norway streets in the city of Boston by the loving hands of four thousand members. This edifice is built as a Testimonial to truth as revealed by divine Love through you to this age. You are hereby most lovingly invited to visit and formally accept this testimonial on the 20th day of February, 1895, at high noon.

"The First Church of Christ, Scientist, at Boston, Mass.

"To the Rev. Mary Baker Eddy.

"By Edward P. Bates

"Caroline S. Bates.

"Boston, January 6, 1895."

Attached by a white ribbon to the scroll is a gold key to the church door. The testimonial is encased in a white satin lined box of rich green velvet. The scroll is on exhibition in the window of J.C. Derby's jewelry store.

(*The Union Signal*, Chicago.)

EXTRACT.

THE NEW WOMAN AND THE NEW CHURCH.

The dedication, in Boston, of a Christian Science temple costing over two hundred thousand dollars, and for which the money was all paid in so that no debt had to be taken care of on dedication day, is a notable event. While we are not, and never have been, devotees of Christian Science, it becomes us as students of public questions not to ignore a movement which starting fifteen years ago has already gained to itself adherents in every part of the civilized world, for it is a significant fact that one cannot take up a daily paper in town or village—to say nothing of cities—'Without seeing notices of Christian Science meetings, and in most instances they are held at "headquarters."

We believe there are two reasons for this remarkable development, which has shown a vitality so unexpected. The first is that a revolt was inevitable from the crass materialism of the cruder science that had taken possession of men's minds, for as a wicked but witty writer has said, "If there were no God we should be obliged to invent one." There is something in the constitution of man that requires the religious sentiment as much as his lungs call for breath; indeed, the breath of his soul is a belief in God.

But when Christian Science arose, the thought of the world's scientific leaders had become materialistically "lopsided," and this condition can never long continue. There must be a righting-up of the mind as surely as of a ship when under stress of storm it is ready to capsize. The pendulum that has swung to one extreme will surely find the other. The religious sentiment in women is so strong that the revolt was headed by them; this was inevitable in the nature of the case. It began in the most intellectual city of the freest country in the world—that is to say, it sought the line of least resistance. Boston is emphatically the women's paradise, numerically, socially, indeed, every way. Here they have the largest individuality, the most recognition, the widest outlook. Mrs. Eddy we have never seen; her book has many a time been sent to us by interested friends and out of respect to them we have fairly broken our mental teeth over its granitic pebbles. That we could not understand it might be rather to the credit of the book than otherwise. On this subject we have no opinion to pronounce, but simply state the fact.

We do not, therefore, speak of the system it sets forth, either to praise or blame, but this much is true; the spirit of Christian Science ideas has caused an army of well meaning people to believe in God and the power of faith, who did not believe in them before. It has made a myriad of women more thoughtful and devout; it has brought a hopeful spirit into the homes of unnumbered invalids. The belief that "thoughts are things," that the invisible is the only real world, that we are here to be trained into harmony with the laws of God, and that what we are here determines where we shall be hereafter—all these ideas are Christian.

The chimes on the Christian Science temple in Boston played "All hail the power of Jesus' name," on the morning of the dedication. We did not attend, but we learn that the name of Christ is nowhere spoken with more reverence than it was during those services, and that He is set forth as the power of God for righteousness and the express image of God for love.

(*The New Century*, Boston, February, 1885.)

ONE POINT OF VIEW.—THE NEW WOMAN.

We all know her—she is simply the woman of the past with an added grace—a newer charm. Some of her dearest ones call her "selfish" because she thinks so much of herself she spends her whole time helping others. She represents the composite beauty, sweetness, and nobility of all those who scorn self for the sake of Love and her handmaiden Duty—of all those who seek the brightness of truth not as the moth to be destroyed thereby, but as the lark who soars and sings to the great sun. She is of those who have so much to give they want no time to take, and their name is legion. She is as full of beautiful possibilities as a perfect harp, and she realizes that all the harmonies of the universe are in herself, while her own soul plays upon magic strings the unwritten anthems of love. She is the apostle of the true, the beautiful, the good, commissioned to complete all that the twelve have left undone. Hers is the mission of missions—the highest of all—to make the body not the prison, but the palace of the soul, with the brain for its great white throne.

When she comes like the south wind into the cold haunts of sin and sorrow her words are smiles and her smiles are the sunlight which heals the stricken soul. Her hand is tender—but steel tempered with holy resolve, and as one whom her love had glorified once said—she is soft and gentle, but you could no more turn her from her course than winter could stop the coming of spring. She has long learned with patience, and to-day she knows many things dear to the soul far better than her teachers. In olden times the Jews claimed to be the conservators of the world's morals—they treated woman as a chattel, and said that because she was created after man, she was created solely for man. Too many still are Jews who never called Abraham "Father," while the Jews themselves have long acknowledged woman as man's proper helpmeet. In those days women had few lawful claims and no one to urge them. True, there were Miriam and Esther, but they sang and sacrificed for their people, not for their sex. To-day there are ten thousand Esthers, and Miriams by the million, who sing best by singing most for their own sex. They are demanding the right to help make the laws, or at least to help enforce the laws upon which depends the welfare of their husbands, their children, and themselves. Why should our selfish self longer remain deaf to their cry? The date is no longer B.C. Might no longer makes right, and in this fair land at least fear has ceased to kiss the iron heel of wrong. Why then should we continue to demand woman's love and woman's help while we recklessly promise as lover and candidate what we never fulfill as husband and office-holder? In our secret heart our better self is shamed and dishonored, and appeals from Philip drunk to Philip sober, but has not yet the moral strength and courage to prosecute the appeal. But the east is rosy and the sunlight cannot long be delayed. Woman must not and will not be disheartened by a thousand denials or a million of broken pledges. With the assurance of faith she prays, with the certainty of inspiration she works, and with the patience of genius she waits. At last she is becoming "as fair as the morn, as bright as the sun, and as terrible as an army with banners" to those who march under the black flag of oppression and wield the ruthless sword of injustice.

In olden times it was the Amazons who conquered the invincibles, and we must look now to their daughters to overcome our own allied armies of evil and to save us from ourselves. She must and will succeed, for as David sang—"God shall help her and that right early." When we try to praise her later works it is as if we would pour incense upon the rose. It is the proudest boast of many of us that we are "bound to her by bonds dearer than freedom," and that we live in the reflected royalty which shines from her brow. We rejoice with her that at last we begin to know what John on Patmos meant—"And there appeared a great wonder in Heaven, a woman clothed with the sun, and the moon under her feet, and upon her head a crown of twelve stars." She brought to warring men the Prince of Peace, and He, departing, left His scepter not in her hand, but in her soul. "The time of times" is near when "the new woman" shall subdue the whole earth with the weapons of peace. Then shall wrong be robbed of her bitterness and ingratitude of her sting; revenge shall clasp hands with pity, and love shall dwell in the tents of hate, while side by side, equal partners in all that is worth living for, shall stand the new man with the new woman.

(*Christian Science Journal,* January, 1895.)

EXTRACT.

THE MOTHER CHURCH.

The Mother Church edifice—The First Church of Christ, Scientist, in Boston, is erected. The close of the year Anno Domini, 1894, witnessed the completion of "our Prayer in Stone," all predictions and prognostications to the contrary notwithstanding.

Of the significance of this achievement we shall not undertake to speak in this article. It can be better felt than expressed. All who are awake thereto have some measure of understanding of what it means. But only the future will tell the story of its mighty meaning or unfold it to the comprehension of mankind. It is enough for us now to know that all obstacles to its completion have been met and overcome, and that our temple is completed as God intended it should be.

This achievement is the result of long years of untiring, unselfish, and zealous effort on the part of our beloved Teacher and Leader, the Reverend Mary Baker Eddy, the Discoverer and Founder of Christian Science, who nearly thirty years ago began to lay the foundation of this temple, and whose devotion and consecration to God and humanity during the intervening years have made its erection possible.

Those who now, in part, understand her mission, turn their hearts in gratitude to her for her great work, and those who do not understand it will, in the fulness of time, see and acknowledge it. In the measure in which she has unfolded and demonstrated Divine Love and built up in human consciousness a better and higher conception of God as Life, Truth, and Love,—as the Divine Principle of all things which really exist,—and in the degree in which she has demonstrated the system of healing of Jesus and the Apostles, surely she, as the one chosen of God to this end, is entitled to the gratitude and love of all who desire a better and grander humanity, and who believe it to be possible to establish the Kingdom of Heaven upon earth in accordance with the prayer and teachings of Jesus Christ.

(*Concord Evening Monitor*, March 23, 1895.)

TESTIMONIAL AND GIFT.

To Rev. Mary Baker Eddy, from The First Church of Christ, Scientist, in Boston.

Rev. Mary Baker Eddy received Friday, from the Christian Science board of directors, Boston, a beautiful and unique testimonial of the appreciation of her labors and loving generosity in the cause of their common faith. It was a facsimile of the corner-stone of the new church of the Christian Scientists, just completed, being of granite, about six inches in each dimension, and contains a solid gold box, upon the cover of which is this inscription:

"To our Beloved Teacher, the Reverend Mary Baker Eddy, Discoverer and Founder of Christian Science, from her affectionate Students, the Christian Science Board of Directors." On the under side of the cover are the facsimile signatures of the directors, Ira O. Knapp, William B. Johnson, Joseph Armstrong, and Stephen A. Chase, with the date, "1895." The beautiful souvenir is encased in an elegant plush box.

Accompanying the stone testimonial was the following address from the board of directors:

BOSTON, March 20, 1895.

To the Reverend Mary Baker Eddy, our beloved teacher and leader:

We are happy to announce to you the completion of The First Church of Christ, Scientist, in Boston.

In behalf of your loving students and all contributors wherever they may be, we hereby present this church to you as a testimonial of love and gratitude for your labors and loving sacrifice, as the discoverer and founder of Christian Science, and the author of its text-book, "SCIENCE AND HEALTH WITH KEY To THE SCRIPTURES."

We therefore respectfully extend to you the invitation to become the permanent pastor of this church, in connection with the Bible, and the Book alluded to above, which you have already ordained as our pastor. And we most cordially invite you to be present and take charge of any services that may be held therein. We especially desire you to be present on the twenty-fourth day of March, eighteen hundred and ninety-five, to accept this offering, with our humble benediction.

Lovingly yours,

IRA O. KNAPP,
WILLIAM B. JOHNSON,
JOSEPH ARMSTRONG,
STEPHEN A. CHASE,
The Christian Science Board of Directors.

REV. MRS. EDDY'S REPLY.
BELOVED DIRECTORS AND BRETHREN:—

For your costly offering, and kind call to the pastorate of "The First Church of Christ, Scientist," in Boston—accept my profound thanks. But permit me, respectfully, to decline their acceptance, while I fully appreciate your kind intentions.-If it will comfort you in the least, make me your Pastor *Emeritus*, nominally. Through my book, your text-book, I already speak to you each Sunday. You ask too much when asking me to accept your grand Church edifice. I have more of earth now, than I desire, and less of heaven; so pardon my refusal of that as a material offering. More effectual than the forum are our states of mind, to bless mankind. This wish stops not with my pen—God give you grace. As our Church's tall tower detains the sun, so, may luminous lines from your lives, linger, a legacy to our race.

MARY BAKER EDDY.

March 25, 1895.

From Canada to New Orleans, and from the Atlantic to the Pacific ocean, the author has received leading newspapers with uniformly kind and interesting articles on the dedication of the Mother church. They were, however, too voluminous for these pages. Those were copied, and she could append only a few of the names of other prominent newspapers whose articles were reluctantly omitted.

LIST OF LEADING NEWSPAPERS WHOSE ARTICLES ARE OMITTED.

EASTERN STATES.

Advertiser, Calais, Me.
Advertiser, Boston, Mass.
Farmer, Bridgeport, Conn.
Independent, Rockland, Mass.
Kennebec Journal, Augusta, Me.
News, New Haven, Conn.
News, Newport, R.I.
Post, Boston, Mass.
Post, Hartford, Conn.
Republican, Springfield, Mass.
Sentinel, Eastport, Me.
Sun, Attleboro, Mass.

MIDDLE STATES.

Advertiser, New York City.
Bulletin, Auburn, N.Y.
Daily, York, Pa.
Enquirer, Philadelphia, Pa.
Evening Reporter, Lebanon, Pa.
Farmer, Bridgeport, N.Y.
Herald, Rochester, N.Y.
Independent, Harrisburg, Pa.
Independent, New York City.
Journal, Lockport, N.Y.
Knickerbocker, Albany, N.Y.
News, Buffalo, N.Y.
News, Newark, N.J.
Once A Week, New York City.
Post, Pittsburg, Pa.
Press, Albany, N.Y.
Press, New York City.
Press, Philadelphia, Pa.
Saratogian, Saratoga Springs, N.Y.
Sun, New York City.
Telegram, Philadelphia, Pa.
Telegram, Troy, N.Y.
Times, Trenton, N.J.

SOUTHERN STATES.

Commercial, Louisville, Ky.
Journal, Atlanta, Ga.
Post, Washington, D.C.
Telegram, New Orleans, La.
Times, New Orleans, La.
Times-Herald, Dallas, Tex.

WESTERN STATES.

Bee, Omaha, Neb.
Bulletin, San Francisco, Cal.
Chronicle, San Francisco, Cal.
Mite, Chicago, Ill.
Enquirer, Oakland, Cal.
Free Press, Detroit, Mich.
Gazette, Burlington, Iowa.
Herald, Grand Rapids, Mich.
Herald, St. Joseph, Mo.
Journal, Columbus, Ohio.
Journal, Topeka, Kans.
Leader, Bloomington, Ill.
Leader, Cleveland, Ohio.
News, St. Joseph, Mo.
News-Tribune, Duluth, Minn.
Pioneer-Press, St. Paul, Minn.
Post-Intelligencer, Seattle, Wash.
Salt Lake Herald, Salt Lake City, Utah.
Sentinel, Indianapolis, Ind.
Sentinel, Milwaukee, Wis.
Star, Kansas City, Mo.
Telegram, Portland, Ore.
Times, Chicago, Ill.
Times, Minneapolis, Minn.
Tribune, Minneapolis, Minn.
Tribune, Salt Lake City, Utah.
Free Press, London, Can.

RETROSPECTION
AND

INTROSPECTION

BY

MARY BAKER EDDY

AUTHOR OF SCIENCE AND HEALTH WITH
KEY TO THE SCRIPTURES

84

CONTENTS

RETROSPECTION AND INTROSPECTION

ANCESTRAL SHADOWS

My ancestors, according to the flesh, were from both Scotland and England, my great-grandfather, on my father's side, being John McNeil of Edinburgh.

His wife, my great-grandmother, was Marion Moor, and her family is said to have been in some way related to Hannah More, the pious and popular English authoress of a century ago.

I remember reading, in my childhood, certain manuscripts containing Scriptural sonnets, besides other verses and enigmas which my grandmother said were written by my great-grandmother. But because my great-grandmother wrote a stray sonnet and an occasional riddle, it was no sign that she inherited a spark from Hannah More, or was her relative.

John and Marion Moor McNeil had a daughter, who perpetuated her mother's name. This second Marion McNeil in due time was married to an Englishman, named Joseph Baker, and so became my paternal grandmother, the Scotch and English elements thus mingling in her children.

Mrs. Marion McNeil Baker was reared among the Scotch Covenanters, and had in her character that sturdy Calvinistic devotion to Protestant liberty which gave those religionists the poetic daring and pious picturesqueness which we find so graphically set forth in the pages of Sir Walter Scott and in John Wilson's sketches.

Joseph Baker and his wife, Marion McNeil, came to America seeking "freedom to worship God;" though they could hardly have crossed the Atlantic more than a score of years prior to the Revolutionary period.

With them they brought to New England a heavy sword, encased in a brass scabbard, on which was inscribed the name of a kinsman upon whom the weapon had been bestowed by Sir William Wallace, from whose patriotism and bravery comes that heart-stirring air, "Scots wha hae wi' Wallace bled."

My childhood was also gladdened by one of my Grandmother Baker's books, printed in olden type and replete with the phraseology current in the seventeenth and eighteenth centuries.

Among grandmother's treasures were some newspapers, yellow with age. Some of these, however, were not very ancient, nor had they crossed the ocean; for they were American newspapers, one of which contained a full account of the death and burial of George Washington.

A relative of my Grandfather Baker was General Henry Knox of Revolutionary fame. I was fond of listening, when a child, to grandmother's stories about General Knox, for whom she cherished a high regard.

In the line of my Grandmother Baker's family was the late Sir John Macneill, a Scotch knight, who was prominent in British politics, and at one time held the position of ambassador to Persia.

My grandparents were likewise connected with Capt. John Lovewell of Dunstable, New Hampshire, whose gallant leadership and death, in the Indian troubles of 1722-1725, caused that prolonged contest to be known historically as Lovewell's War.

A cousin of my grandmother was John Macneil, the New Hampshire general who fought at Lundy's Lane, and won distinction in 1814 at the neighboring battle of Chippewa, towards the close of the War of 1812.

AUTOBIOGRAPHIC REMINISCENCES

This venerable grandmother had thirteen children, the youngest of whom was my father, Mark Baker, who inherited the homestead, and with his brother, James Baker, he inherited my grandfather's farm of about five hundred acres, lying in the adjoining towns of Concord and Bow, in the State of New Hampshire.

One hundred acres of the old farm are still cultivated and owned by Uncle James Baker's grandson, brother of the Hon. Henry Moore Baker of Washington, D.C.

The farm-house, situated on the summit of a hill, commanded a broad picturesque view of the Merrimac River and the undulating lands of three townships. But change has been busy. Where once stretched broad fields of bending grain waving gracefully in the sunlight, and orchards of apples, peaches, pears, and cherries shone richly in the mellow hues of autumn,—now the lone night-bird cries, the crow caws cautiously, and wandering winds sigh low requiems through dark pine groves. Where green pastures bright with berries, singing brooklets, beautiful wild flowers, and flecked with large flocks and herds, covered areas of rich acres,—now the scrub-oak, poplar, and fern flourish.

The wife of Mark Baker was Abigail Barnard Ambrose, daughter of Deacon Nathaniel Ambrose of Pembroke, a small town situated near Concord, just across the bridge, on the left bank of the Merrimac River.

Grandfather Ambrose was a very religious man, and gave the money for erecting the first Congregational Church in Pembroke.

In the Baker homestead at Bow I was born, the youngest of my parents' six children and the object of their tender solicitude.

During my childhood my parents removed to Tilton, eighteen miles from Concord, and there the family remained until the names of both father and mother were inscribed on the stone memorials in the Park Cemetery of that beautiful village.

My father possessed a strong intellect and an iron will. Of my mother I cannot speak as I would, for memory recalls qualities to which the pen can never do justice. The following is a brief extract from the eulogy of the Rev. Richard S. Rust, D.D., who for many years had resided in Tilton and knew my sainted mother in all the walks of life.

The character of Mrs. Abigail Ambrose Baker was distinguished for numerous excellences. She possessed a strong intellect, a

sympathizing heart, and a placid spirit. Her presence, like the
gentle dew and cheerful light, was felt by all around her. She
gave an elevated character to the tone of conversation in the
circles in which she moved, and directed attention to themes at
once pleasing and profitable.

As a mother, she was untiring in her efforts to secure the
happiness of her family. She ever entertained a lively sense of
the parental obligation, especially in regard to the education of
her children. The oft-repeated impressions of that sainted spirit,
on the hearts of those especially entrusted to her watch-care, can
never be effaced, and can hardly fail to induce them to follow her
to the brighter world. Her life was a living illustration of
Christian faith.

My childhood's home I remember as one with the open hand. The needy
were ever welcome, and to the clergy were accorded special household
privileges.

Among the treasured reminiscences of my much respected parents, brothers,
and sisters, is the memory of my second brother, Albert Baker, who was, next to
my mother, the very dearest of my kindred. To speak of his beautiful character
as I cherish it, would require more space than this little book can afford.

My brother Albert was graduated at Dartmouth College in 1834, and was
reputed one of the most talented, close, and thorough scholars ever connected
with that institution. For two or three years he read law at Hillsborough, in the
office of Franklin Pierce, afterwards President of the United States; but later
Albert spent a year in the office of the Hon. Richard Fletcher of Boston. He was
consequently admitted to the bar in two States, Massachusetts and New
Hampshire. In 1837 he succeeded to the law-office which Mr. Pierce had
occupied, and was soon elected to the Legislature of his native State, where he
served the public interests faithfully for two consecutive years. Among other
important bills which were carried through the Legislature by his persistent
energy was one for the abolition of imprisonment for debt.

In 1841 he received further political preferment, by nomination to Congress
on a majority vote of seven thousand,—it was the largest vote of the State; but
he passed away at the age of thirty-one, after a short illness, before his election.
His noble political antagonist, the Hon. Isaac Hill, of Concord, wrote of my
brother as follows:—

Albert Baker was a young man of uncommon promise. Gifted with the
highest order of intellectual powers, he trained and schooled them
by intense and almost incessant study throughout his short life.
He was fond of investigating abstruse and metaphysical principles,
and he never forsook them until he had explored their every nook
and corner, however hidden and remote. Had life and health been

spared to him, he would have made himself one of the most distinguished men in the country. As a lawyer he was able and learned, and in the successful practice of a very large business. He was noted for his boldness and firmness, and for his powerful advocacy of the side he deemed right. His death will be deplored, with the most poignant grief, by a large number of friends, who expected no more than they realized from his talents and acquirements. This sad event will not be soon forgotten. It blights too many hopes; it carries with it too much of sorrow and loss. It is a public calamity.

VOICES NOT OUR OWN

Many peculiar circumstances and events connected with my childhood throng the chambers of memory. For some twelve months, when I was about eight years old, I repeatedly heard a voice, calling me distinctly by name, three times, in an ascending scale. I thought this was my mother's voice, and sometimes went to her, beseeching her to tell me what she wanted. Her answer was always, "Nothing, child! What do you mean?" Then I would say, "Mother, who *did* call me? I heard somebody call *Mary*, three times!" This continued until I grew discouraged, and my mother was perplexed and anxious.

One day, when my cousin, Mehitable Huntoon, was visiting us, and I sat in a little chair by her side, in the same room with grandmother,—the call again came, so loud that Mehitable heard it, though I had ceased to notice it. Greatly surprised, my cousin turned to me and said, "Your mother is calling you!" but I answered not, till again the same call was thrice repeated. Mehitable then said sharply, "Why don't you go? your mother is calling you!" I then left the room, went to my mother, and once more asked her if she had summoned me? She answered as always before. Then I earnestly declared my cousin had heard the voice, and said that mother wanted me. Accordingly she returned with me to grandmother's room, and led my cousin into an adjoining apartment. The door was ajar, and I listened with bated breath. Mother told Mehitable all about this mysterious voice, and asked if she really did hear Mary's name pronounced in audible tones. My cousin answered quickly, and emphasized her affirmation.

That night, before going to rest, my mother read to me the Scriptural narrative of little Samuel, and bade me, when the voice called again, to reply as he did, "Speak, Lord; for Thy servant heareth." The voice came; but I was afraid, and did not answer. Afterward I wept, and prayed that God would forgive me, resolving to do, next time, as my mother had bidden me. When the call came again I did answer, in the words of Samuel, but never again to the material senses was that mysterious call repeated.

Is it not much that I may worship Him,
  With naught my spirit's breathings to control,
And feel His presence in the vast and dim

And whispering woods, where dying thunders roll
From the far cataracts? Shall I not rejoice
That I have learned at last to know His voice
From man's?—I will rejoice! My soaring soul
Now hath redeemed her birthright of the day,
And won, through clouds, to Him, her own unfettered way!
—MRS. HEMANS.

EARLY STUDIES

My father was taught to believe that my brain was too large for my body and so kept me much out of school, but I gained book-knowledge with far less labor than is usually requisite. At ten years of age I was as familiar with Lindley Murray's Grammar as with the Westminster Catechism; and the latter I had to repeat every Sunday. My favorite studies were natural philosophy, logic, and moral science. From my brother Albert I received lessons in the ancient tongues, Hebrew, Greek, and Latin. My brother studied Hebrew during his college vacations. After my discovery of Christian Science, most of the knowledge I had gleaned from schoolbooks vanished like a dream.

Learning was so illumined, that grammar was eclipsed. Etymology was divine history, voicing the idea of God in man's origin and signification. Syntax was spiritual order and unity. Prosody, the song of angels, and no earthly or inglorious theme.

GIRLHOOD COMPOSITION

From childhood I was a verse-maker. Poetry suited my emotions better than prose. The following is one of my girlhood productions.

ALPHABET AND BAYONET

If fancy plumes aerial flight,
  Go fix thy restless mind
On learning's lore and wisdom's might,
  And live to bless mankind.
The sword is sheathed, 'tis freedom's hour,
  No despot bears misrule,
Where knowledge plants the foot of power
  In our God-blessed free school.

Forth from this fount the streamlets flow,
  That widen in their course.
Hero and sage arise to show
  Science the mighty source,
And laud the land whose talents rock
  The cradle of her power,
And wreaths are twined round Plymouth Rock,
  From erudition's bower.

Farther than feet of chamois fall,
  Free as the generous air,
Strains nobler far than clarion call
  Wake freedom's welcome, where
Minerva's silver sandals still
  Are loosed, and not effete;
Where echoes still my day-dreams thrill,
  Woke by her fancied feet.

THEOLOGICAL REMINISCENCE

At the age of twelve[2] I was admitted to the Congregational (Trinitarian) Church, my parents having been members of that body for a half-century. In connection with this event, some circumstances are noteworthy. Before this step was taken, the doctrine of unconditional election, or predestination, greatly troubled me; for I was unwilling to be saved, if my brothers and sisters were to be numbered among those who were doomed to perpetual banishment from God. So perturbed was I by the thoughts aroused by this erroneous doctrine, that the family doctor was summoned, and pronounced me stricken with fever.

My father's relentless theology emphasized belief in a final judgment-day, in the danger of endless punishment, and in a Jehovah merciless towards unbelievers; and of these things he now spoke, hoping to win me from dreaded heresy.

My mother, as she bathed my burning temples, bade me lean on God's love, which would give me rest, if I went to Him in prayer, as I was wont to do, seeking His guidance. I prayed; and a soft glow of ineffable joy came over me. The fever was gone, and I rose and dressed myself, in a normal condition of health. Mother saw this, and was glad. The physician marvelled; and the

---

[2] See Page 311, Lines 12 to 17, "The First Church of Christ, Scientist, and Miscellany.

"horrible decree" of predestination—as John Calvin rightly called his own tenet—forever lost its power over me.

When the meeting was held for the examination of candidates for membership, I was of course present. The pastor was an old-school expounder of the strictest Presbyterian doctrines. He was apparently as eager to have unbelievers in these dogmas lost, as he was to have elect believers converted and rescued from perdition; for both salvation and condemnation depended, according to his views, upon the good pleasure of infinite Love. However, I was ready for his doleful questions, which I answered without a tremor, declaring that never could I unite with the church, if assent to this doctrine was essential thereto.

Distinctly do I recall what followed. I stoutly maintained that I was willing to trust God, and take my chance of spiritual safety with my brothers and sisters,— not one of whom had then made any profession of religion,—even if my creedal doubts left me outside the doors. The minister then wished me to tell him when I had experienced a change of heart; but tearfully I had to respond that I could not designate any precise time. Nevertheless he persisted in the assertion that I *had* been truly regenerated, and asked me to say how I felt when the new light dawned within me. I replied that I could only answer him in the words of the Psalmist: "Search me, O God, and know my heart: try me, and know my thoughts: and see if there be any wicked way in me, and lead me in the way everlasting."

This was so earnestly said, that even the oldest church-members wept. After the meeting was over they came and kissed me. To the astonishment of many, the good clergyman's heart also melted, and he received me into their communion, and my protest along with me. My connection with this religious body was retained till I founded a church of my own, built on the basis of Christian Science, "Jesus Christ himself being the chief corner-stone."

In confidence of faith, I could say in David's words, "I will go in the strength of the Lord God: I will make mention of Thy righteousness, even of Thine only. O God, Thou hast taught me from my youth: and hitherto have I declared Thy wondrous works." (Psalms lxxi. 16, 17.)

In the year 1878 I was called to preach in Boston at the Baptist Tabernacle of Rev. Daniel C. Eddy, D.D.,—by the pastor of this church. I accepted the invitation and commenced work.

The congregation so increased in number the pews were not sufficient to seat the audience and benches were used in the aisles. At the close of my engagement we parted in Christian fellowship, if not in full unity of doctrine.

Our last vestry meeting was made memorable by eloquent addresses from persons who feelingly testified to having been healed through my preaching. Among other diseases cured they specified cancers. The cases described had been treated and given over by physicians of the popular schools of medicine, but I had not heard of these cases till the persons who divulged their secret joy were healed. A prominent churchman agreeably informed the congregation that many others present had been healed under my preaching, but were too timid to testify in public.

One memorable Sunday afternoon, a soprano,—clear, strong, sympathetic,—floating up from the pews, caught my ear. When the meeting was over, two ladies pushing their way through the crowd reached the platform. With tears of joy flooding her eyes—for she was a mother—one of them said, "Did you hear my daughter sing? Why, she has not sung before since she left the choir and was in consumption! When she entered this church one hour ago she could not speak a loud word, and now, oh, thank God, she is healed!"

It was not an uncommon occurrence in my own church for the sick to be healed by my sermon. Many pale cripples went into the church leaning on crutches who went out carrying them on their shoulders. "And these signs shall follow them that believe."

The charter for The Mother Church in Boston was obtained June, 1879,[3] and the same month the members, twenty-six in number, extended a call to Mary B.G. Eddy to become their pastor. She accepted the call, and was ordained A.D. 1881.

THE COUNTRY-SEAT

Written in youth, while visiting a family friend in the beautiful suburbs of Boston.

Wild spirit of song,—midst the zephyrs at play
In bowers of beauty,—I bend to thy lay,
And woo, while I worship in deep sylvan spot,
The Muses' soft echoes to kindle the grot.
Wake chords of my lyre, with musical kiss,
To vibrate and tremble with accents of bliss.

Here morning peers out, from her crimson repose,
On proud Prairie Queen and the modest Moss-rose;
And vesper reclines—when the dewdrop is shed
On the heart of the pink—in its odorous bed;
But Flora has stolen the rainbow and sky,
To sprinkle the flowers with exquisite dye.

---

[3] This statement appears to be based upon the Annual Report of the Secretary of The Christian Scientist Association, read at its meeting, January 15, 1880, in which June is named as the month in which the charter for The Mother Church was obtained, instead of August 23, 1879, the correct date.

Here fame-honored hickory rears his bold form,
    And bares a brave breast to the lightning and storm,
    While palm, bay, and laurel, in classical glee,
    Chase tulip, magnolia, and fragrant fringe-tree;
    And sturdy horse-chestnut for centuries hath given
    Its feathery blossom and branches to heaven.

    Here is life! Here is youth! Here the poet's world-wish,—
    Cool waters at play with the gold-gleaming fish;
    While cactus a mellower glory receives
    From light colored softly by blossom and leaves;
    And nestling alder is whispering low,
    In lap of the pear-tree, with musical flow.[4]

Dark sentinel hedgerow is guarding repose,
    Midst grotto and songlet and streamlet that flows
    Where beauty and perfume from buds burst away,
    And ope their closed cells to the bright, laughing day;
    Yet, dwellers in Eden, earth yields you her tear,—
    Oft plucked for the banquet, but laid on the bier.

Earth's beauty and glory delude as the shrine
    Or fount of real joy and of visions divine;
    But hope, as the eaglet that spurneth the sod,
    May soar above matter, to fasten on God,
    And freely adore all His spirit hath made,
    Where rapture and radiance and glory ne'er fade.

Oh, give me the spot where affection may dwell
    In sacred communion with home's magic spell!
    Where flowers of feeling are fragrant and fair,
    And those we most love find a happiness rare;
    But clouds are a presage,—they darken my lay:
    This life is a shadow, and hastens away.

---

[4] An alder growing from the bent branch of a pear-tree.

MARRIAGE AND PARENTAGE

In 1843 I was united to my first husband, Colonel George Washington Glover of Charleston, South Carolina, the ceremony taking place under the paternal roof in Tilton.

After parting with the dear home circle I went with him to the South; but he was spared to me for only one brief year. He was in Wilmington, North Carolina, on business, when the yellow-fever raged in that city, and was suddenly attacked by this insidious disease, which in his case proved fatal.

My husband was a freemason, being a member in Saint Andrew's Lodge, Number 10, and of Union Chapter, Number 3, of Royal Arch masons. He was highly esteemed and sincerely lamented by a large circle of friends and acquaintances, whose kindness and sympathy helped to support me in this terrible bereavement. A month later I returned to New Hampshire, where, at the end of four months, my babe was born.

Colonel Glover's tender devotion to his young bride was remarked by all observers. With his parting breath he gave pathetic directions to his brother masons about accompanying her on her sad journey to the North. Here it is but justice to record, they performed their obligations most faithfully.

After returning to the paternal roof I lost all my husband's property, except what money I had brought with me; and remained with my parents until after my mother's decease.

A few months before my father's second marriage, to Mrs. Elizabeth Patterson Duncan, sister of Lieutenant-Governor George W. Patterson of New York, my little son, about four years of age, was sent away from me, and put under the care of our family nurse, who had married, and resided in the northern part of New Hampshire. I had no training for self-support, and my home I regarded as very precious. The night before my child was taken from me, I knelt by his side throughout the dark hours, hoping for a vision of relief from this trial. The following lines are taken from my poem, "Mother's Darling," written after this separation:—

Thy smile through tears, as sunshine o'er the sea,
  Awoke new beauty in the surge's roll!
Oh, life is dead, bereft of all, with thee,—
  Star of my earthly hope, babe of my soul.

My second marriage was very unfortunate, and from it I was compelled to ask for a bill of divorce, which was granted me in the city of Salem, Massachusetts.

My dominant thought in marrying again was to get back my child, but after our marriage his stepfather was not willing he should have a home with me. A plot was consummated for keeping us apart. The family to whose care he was committed very soon removed to what was then regarded as the Far West.

After his removal a letter was read to my little son, informing him that his mother was dead and buried. Without my knowledge a guardian was appointed him, and I was then informed that my son was lost. Every means within my power was employed to find him, but without success. We never met again until he had reached the age of thirty-four, had a wife and two children, and by a strange providence had learned that his mother still lived, and came to see me in Massachusetts.

Meanwhile he had served as a volunteer throughout the war for the Union, and at its expiration was appointed United States Marshal of the Territory of Dakota.

It is well to know, dear reader, that our material, mortal history is but the record of dreams, not of man's real existence, and the dream has no place in the Science of being. It is "as a tale that is told," and "as the shadow when it declineth." The heavenly intent of earth's shadows is to chasten the affections, to rebuke human consciousness and turn it gladly from a material, false sense of life and happiness, to spiritual joy and true estimate of being.

The awakening from a false sense of life, substance, and mind in matter, is as yet imperfect; but for those lucid and enduring lessons of Love which tend to this result, I bless God.

Mere historic incidents and personal events are frivolous and of no moment, unless they illustrate the ethics of Truth. To this end, but only to this end, such narrations may be admissible and advisable; but if spiritual conclusions are separated from their premises, the *nexus* is lost, and the argument, with its rightful conclusions, becomes correspondingly obscure. The human history needs to be revised, and the material record expunged.

The Gospel narratives bear brief testimony even to the life of our great Master. His spiritual noumenon and phenomenon silenced portraiture. Writers less wise than the apostles essayed in the Apocryphal New Testament a legendary and traditional history of the early life of Jesus. But St. Paul summarized the character of Jesus as the model of Christianity, in these words: "Consider him that endured such contradiction of sinners against himself." "Who for the joy that was set before him endured the cross, despising the shame, and is set down at the right hand of the throne of God."

It may be that the mortal life-battle still wages, and must continue till its involved errors are vanquished by victory-bringing Science; but this triumph will come! God is over all. He alone is our origin, aim, and being. The real man is not of the dust, nor is he ever created through the flesh; for his father and mother are the one Spirit, and his brethren are all the children of one parent, the eternal good.

EMERGENCE INTO LIGHT

The trend of human life was too eventful to leave me undisturbed in the illusion that this so-called life could be a real and abiding rest. All things earthly must ultimately yield to the irony of fate, or else be merged into the one infinite Love.

As these pungent lessons became clearer, they grew sterner. Previously the cloud of mortal mind seemed to have a silver lining; but now it was not even fringed with light. Matter was no longer spanned with its rainbow of promise. The world was dark. The oncoming hours were indicated by no floral dial. The senses could not prophesy sunrise or starlight.

Thus it was when the moment arrived of the heart's bridal to more spiritual existence. When the door opened, I was waiting and watching; and, lo, the bridegroom came! The character of the Christ was illuminated by the midnight torches of Spirit. My heart knew its Redeemer. He whom my affections had diligently sought was as the One "altogether lovely," as "the chiefest," the only, "among ten thousand." Soulless famine had fled. Agnosticism, pantheism, and theosophy were void. Being was beautiful, its substance, cause, and currents were God and His idea. I had touched the hem of Christian Science.

THE GREAT DISCOVERY

It was in Massachusetts, in February, 1866, and after the death of the magnetic doctor, Mr. P.P. Quimby, whom spiritualists would associate therewith, but who was in no wise connected with this event, that I discovered the Science of divine metaphysical healing which I afterwards named Christian Science. The discovery came to pass in this way. During twenty years prior to my discovery I had been trying to trace all physical effects to a mental cause; and in the latter part of 1866 I gained the scientific certainty that all causation was Mind, and every effect a mental phenomenon.

My immediate recovery from the effects of an injury caused by an accident, an injury that neither medicine nor surgery could reach, was the falling apple that led me to the discovery how to be well myself, and how to make others so.

Even to the homoeopathic physician who attended me, and rejoiced in my recovery, I could not then explain the *modus* of my relief. I could only assure him that the divine Spirit had wrought the miracle—a miracle which later I found to be in perfect scientific accord with divine law.

I then withdrew from society about three years,—to ponder my mission, to search the Scriptures, to find the Science of Mind that should take the things of God and show them to the creature, and reveal the great curative Principle,— Deity.

The Bible was my textbook. It answered my questions as to how I was healed; but the Scriptures had to me a new meaning, a new tongue. Their spiritual signification appeared; and I apprehended for the first time, in their spiritual meaning, Jesus' teaching and demonstration, and the Principle and rule of spiritual Science and metaphysical healing,—in a word, Christian Science.

I named it *Christian*, because it is compassionate, helpful, and spiritual. God I called *immortal Mind*. That which sins, suffers, and dies, I named *mortal mind*. The physical senses, or sensuous nature, I called *error* and *shadow*. Soul I denominated *substance*, because Soul alone is truly substantial. God I characterized as individual entity, but His corporeality I denied. The real I claimed as eternal; and its antipodes, or the temporal, I described as unreal. Spirit I called the *reality*; and matter, the *unreality*.

I knew the human conception of God to be that He was a physically personal being, like unto man; and that the five physical senses are so many witnesses to the physical personality of mind and the real existence of matter; but I learned that these material senses testify falsely, that matter neither sees, hears, nor feels Spirit, and is therefore inadequate to form any proper conception of the infinite Mind. "If I bear witness of myself, my witness is not true." (John v. 31.)

I beheld with ineffable awe our great Master's purpose in not questioning those he healed as to their disease or its symptoms, and his marvellous skill in demanding neither obedience to hygienic laws, nor prescribing drugs to support the divine power which heals. Adoringly I discerned the Principle of his holy heroism and Christian example on the cross, when he refused to drink the "vinegar and gall," a preparation of poppy, or aconite, to allay the tortures of crucifixion.

Our great Way-shower, steadfast to the end in his obedience to God's laws, demonstrated for all time and peoples the supremacy of good over evil, and the superiority of Spirit over matter.

The miracles recorded in the Bible, which had before seemed to me supernatural, grew divinely natural and apprehensible; though uninspired interpreters ignorantly pronounce Christ's healing miraculous, instead of seeing therein the operation of the divine law.

Jesus of Nazareth was a natural and divine Scientist. He was so before the material world saw him. He who antedated Abraham, and gave the world a new date in the Christian era, was a Christian Scientist, who needed no discovery of the Science of being in order to rebuke the evidence. To one "born of the flesh," however, divine Science must be a discovery. Woman must give it birth. It must be begotten of spirituality, since none but the pure in heart can see God,—the Principle of all things pure; and none but the "poor in spirit" could first state this Principle, could know yet more of the nothingness of matter and the allness of Spirit, could utilize Truth, and absolutely reduce the demonstration of being, in Science, to the apprehension of the age.

I wrote also, at this period, comments on the Scriptures, setting forth their spiritual interpretation, the Science of the Bible, and so laid the foundation of my work called Science and Health, published in 1875.

If these notes and comments, which have never been read by any one but myself, were published, it would show that after my discovery of the absolute Science of Mind-healing, like all great truths, this spiritual Science developed itself to me until Science and Health was written. These early comments are valuable to me as waymarks of progress, which I would not have effaced.

Up to that time I had not fully voiced my discovery. Naturally, my first jottings were but efforts to express in feeble diction Truth's ultimate. In Longfellow's language,—

But the feeble hands and helpless,
Groping blindly in the darkness,
Touch God's right hand in that darkness,
And are lifted up and strengthened.

As sweet music ripples in one's first thoughts of it like the brooklet in its meandering midst pebbles and rocks, before the mind can duly express it to the ear,—so the harmony of divine Science first broke upon my sense, before gathering experience and confidence to articulate it. Its natural manifestation is beautiful and euphonious, but its written expression increases in power and perfection under the guidance of the great Master.

The divine hand led me into a new world of light and Life, a fresh universe—old to God, but new to His "little one." It became evident that the divine Mind alone must answer, and be found as the Life, or Principle, of all being; and that one must acquaint himself with God, if he would be at peace. He must be ours practically, guiding our every thought and action; else we cannot understand the omnipresence of good sufficiently to demonstrate, even in part, the Science of the perfect Mind and divine healing.

I had learned that thought must be spiritualized, in order to apprehend Spirit. It must become honest, unselfish, and pure, in order to have the least understanding of God in divine Science. The first must become last. Our reliance upon material things must be transferred to a perception of and dependence on spiritual things. For Spirit to be supreme in demonstration, it must be supreme in our affections, and we must be clad with divine power. Purity, self-renunciation, faith, and understanding must reduce all things real to their own mental denomination, Mind, which divides, subdivides, increases, diminishes, constitutes, and sustains, according to the law of God.

I had learned that Mind reconstructed the body, and that nothing else could. How it was done, the spiritual Science of Mind must reveal. It was a mystery to me then, but I have since understood it. All Science is a revelation. Its Principle is divine, not human, reaching higher than the stars of heaven.

Am I a believer in spiritualism? I believe in no *ism*. This is my endeavor, to be a Christian, to assimilate the character and practice of the anointed; and no motive can cause a surrender of this effort. As I understand it, spiritualism is the antipode of Christian Science. I esteem all honest people, and love them, and hold to loving our enemies and doing good to them that "despitefully use you and persecute you."

FOUNDATION WORK

As the pioneer of Christian Science I stood alone in this conflict, endeavoring to smite error with the falchion of Truth. The rare bequests of Christian Science are costly, and they have won fields of battle from which the dainty borrower would have fled. Ceaseless toil, self-renunciation, and love, have cleared its pathway.

The motive of my earliest labors has never changed. It was to relieve the sufferings of humanity by a sanitary system that should include all moral and religious reform.

It is often asked why Christian Science was revealed to me as one intelligence, analyzing, uncovering, and annihilating the false testimony of the physical senses. Why was this conviction necessary to the right apprehension of the invincible and infinite energies of Truth and Love, as contrasted with the foibles and fables of finite mind and material existence.

The answer is plain. St. Paul declared that the law was the schoolmaster, to bring him to Christ. Even so was I led into the mazes of divine metaphysics through the gospel of suffering, the providence of God, and the cross of Christ. No one else can drain the cup which I have drunk to the dregs as the Discoverer and teacher of Christian Science; neither can its inspiration be gained without tasting this cup.

The loss of material objects of affection sunders the dominant ties of earth and points to heaven. Nothing can compete with Christian Science, and its demonstration, in showing this solemn certainty in growing freedom and vindicating "the ways of God" to man. The absolute proof and self-evident propositions of Truth are immeasurably paramount to rubric and dogma in proving the Christ.

From my very childhood I was impelled, by a hunger and thirst after divine things,—a desire for something higher and better than matter, and apart from it,—to seek diligently for the knowledge of God as the one great and ever-present relief from human woe. The first spontaneous motion of Truth and Love, acting through Christian Science on my roused consciousness, banished at once and forever the fundamental error of faith in things material; for this trust is the unseen sin, the unknown foe,—the heart's untamed desire which breaketh the divine commandments. As says St. James: "Whosoever shall keep the whole law, and yet offend in one point, he is guilty of all."

Into mortal mind's material obliquity I gazed, and stood abashed. Blanched was the cheek of pride. My heart bent low before the omnipotence of Spirit, and a tint of humility, soft as the heart of a moonbeam, mantled the earth. Bethlehem and Bethany, Gethsemane and Calvary, spoke to my chastened sense as by the tearful lips of a babe. Frozen fountains were unsealed. Erudite systems of philosophy and religion melted, for Love unveiled the healing promise and potency of a present spiritual *afflatus*. It was the gospel of healing, on its divinely appointed human mission, bearing on its white wings, to my apprehension, "the beauty of holiness,"—even the possibilities of spiritual insight, knowledge, and being.

Early had I learned that whatever is loved materially, as mere corporeal personality, is eventually lost. "For whosoever will save his life shall lose it," said the Master. Exultant hope, if tinged with earthliness, is crushed as the moth.

What is termed mortal and material existence is graphically defined by Calderon, the famous Spanish poet, who wrote,—

What is life? 'Tis but a madness.
  What is life? A mere illusion,
  Fleeting pleasure, fond delusion,
Short-lived joy, that ends in sadness,
  Whose most constant substance seems
  But the dream of other dreams.

MEDICAL EXPERIMENTS

The physical side of this research was aided by hints from homoeopathy, sustaining my final conclusion that mortal belief, instead of the drug, governed the action of material medicine.

I wandered through the dim mazes of *materia medica*, till I was weary of "scientific guessing," as it has been well called. I sought knowledge from the different schools,—allopathy, homoeopathy, hydropathy, electricity, and from various humbugs,—but without receiving satisfaction.

I found, in the two hundred and sixty-two remedies enumerated by Jahr, one pervading secret; namely, that the less material medicine we have, and the more Mind, the better the work is done; a fact which seems to prove the Principle of Mind-healing. One drop of the thirtieth attenuation of *Natrum muriaticum*, in a tumbler-full of water, and one teaspoonful of the water mixed with the faith of ages, would cure patients not affected by a larger dose. The drug disappears in the higher attenuations of homoeopathy, and matter is thereby rarefied to its fatal essence, mortal mind; but immortal Mind, the curative Principle, remains, and is found to be even more active.

The mental virtues of the material methods of medicine, when understood, were insufficient to satisfy my doubts as to the honesty or utility of using a material curative. I must know more of the unmixed, unerring source, in order to gain the Science of Mind, the All-in-all of Spirit, in which matter is obsolete. Nothing less could solve the mental problem. If I sought an answer from the medical schools, the reply was dark and contradictory. Neither ancient nor modern philosophy could clear the clouds, or give me one distinct statement of the spiritual Science of Mind-healing. Human reason was not equal to it.

I claim for healing scientifically the following advantages: *First*: It does away with all material medicines, and recognizes the antidote for all sickness, as well as sin, in the immortal Mind; and mortal mind as the source of all the ills which befall mortals. *Second*: It is more effectual than drugs, and cures when they fail, or only relieve; thus proving the superiority of metaphysics over physics. *Third*: A person healed by Christian Science is not only healed of his disease, but he is advanced morally and spiritually. The mortal body being but the objective state of the mortal mind, this mind must be renovated to improve the body.

FIRST PUBLICATION

In 1870 I copyrighted the first publication on spiritual, scientific Mind-healing, entitled "The Science of Man." This little book is converted into the chapter on Recapitulation in Science and Health. It was so new—the basis it laid down for physical and moral health was so hopelessly original, and men were so unfamiliar with the subject—that I did not venture upon its publication until later, having learned that the merits of Christian Science must be proven before a work on this subject could be profitably published.

The truths of Christian Science are not interpolations of the Scriptures, but the spiritual interpretations thereof. Science is the prism of Truth, which divides its rays and brings out the hues of Deity. Human hypotheses have darkened the glow and grandeur of evangelical religion. When speaking of his true followers in every period, Jesus said, "*They* shall lay hands on the sick, and they shall recover." There is no authority for querying the authenticity of this declaration, for it already was and is demonstrated as practical, and its claim is substantiated,—a claim too immanent to fall to the ground beneath the stroke of artless workmen.

Though a man were girt with the Urim and Thummim of priestly office, and denied the perpetuity of Jesus' command, "Heal the sick," or its application in all time to those who understand Christ as the Truth and the Life, that man would not expound the gospel according to Jesus.

Five years after taking out my first copyright, I taught the Science of Mind-healing, *alias* Christian Science, by writing out my manuscripts for students and distributing them unsparingly. This will account for certain published and unpublished manuscripts extant, which the evil-minded would insinuate did not originate with me.

THE PRECIOUS VOLUME

The first edition of my most important work, Science and Health, containing the complete statement of Christian Science,—the term employed by me to express the divine, or spiritual, Science of Mind-healing, was published in 1875.

When it was first printed, the critics took pleasure in saying, "This book is indeed wholly original, but it will never be read."

The first edition numbered one thousand copies. In September, 1891, it had reached sixty-two editions.

Those who formerly sneered at it, as foolish and eccentric, now declare Bishop Berkeley, David Hume, Ralph Waldo Emerson, or certain German philosophers, to have been the originators of the Science of Mind-healing as therein stated.

Even the Scriptures gave no direct interpretation of the scientific basis for demonstrating the spiritual Principle of healing, until our heavenly Father saw fit, through the Key to the Scriptures, in Science and Health, to unlock this "mystery of godliness."

My reluctance to give the public, in my first edition of Science and Health, the chapter on Animal Magnetism, and the divine purpose that this should be done, may have an interest for the reader, and will be seen in the following circumstances. I had finished that edition as far as that chapter, when the printer informed me that he could not go on with my work. I had already paid him seven hundred dollars, and yet he stopped my work. All efforts to persuade him to finish my book were in vain.

After months had passed, I yielded to a constant conviction that I must insert in my last chapter a partial history of what I had already observed of mental malpractice. Accordingly, I set to work, contrary to my inclination, to fulfil this painful task, and finished my copy for the book. As it afterwards appeared, although I had not thought of such a result, my printer resumed his work at the same time, finished printing the copy he had on hand, and then started for Lynn to see me. The afternoon that he left Boston for Lynn, I started for Boston with my finished copy. We met at the Eastern depot in Lynn, and were both surprised,—I to learn that he had printed all the copy on hand, and had come to tell me he wanted more,—he to find me *en route* for Boston, to give him the closing chapter of my first edition of Science and Health. Not a word had passed between us, audibly or mentally, while this went on. I had grown disgusted with my printer, and become silent. He had come to a standstill through motives and circumstances unknown to me.

Science and Health is the textbook of Christian Science. Whosoever learns the letter of this book, must also gain its spiritual significance, in order to demonstrate Christian Science.

When the demand for this book increased, and people were healed simply by reading it, the copyright was infringed. I entered a suit at law, and my copyright was protected.

RECUPERATIVE INCIDENT

Through four successive years I healed, preached, and taught in a general way, refusing to take any pay for my services and living on a small annuity.

At one time I was called to speak before the Lyceum Club, at Westerly, Rhode Island. On my arrival my hostess told me that her next-door neighbor was dying. I asked permission to see her. It was granted, and with my hostess I went to the invalid's house.

The physicians had given up the case and retired. I had stood by her side about fifteen minutes when the sick woman rose from her bed, dressed herself, and was well. Afterwards they showed me the clothes already prepared for her burial; and told me that her physicians had said the diseased condition was caused by an injury received from a surgical operation at the birth of her last babe, and that it was impossible for her to be delivered of another child. It is sufficient to add her babe was safely born, and weighed twelve pounds. The mother afterwards wrote to me, "I never before suffered so little in childbirth."

This scientific demonstration so stirred the doctors and clergy that they had my notices for a second lecture pulled down, and refused me a hearing in their halls and churches. This circumstance is cited simply to show the opposition which Christian Science encountered a quarter-century ago, as contrasted with its present welcome into the sickroom.

Many were the desperate cases I instantly healed, "without money and without price," and in most instances without even an acknowledgment of the benefit.

A TRUE MAN

My last marriage was with Asa Gilbert Eddy, and was a blessed and spiritual union, solemnized at Lynn, Massachusetts, by the Rev. Samuel Barrett Stewart, in the year 1877. Dr. Eddy was the first student publicly to announce himself a Christian Scientist, and place these symbolic words on his office sign. He forsook all to follow in this line of light. He was the first organizer of a Christian Science Sunday School, which he superintended. He also taught a special Bible-class; and he lectured so ably on Scriptural topics that clergymen of other denominations listened to him with deep interest. He was remarkably successful in Mind-healing, and untiring in his chosen work. In 1882 he passed away, with a smile of peace and love resting on his serene countenance. "Mark the perfect *man*, and behold the upright: for the end of *that* man *is* peace." (Psalms xxxvii. 37.)

COLLEGE AND CHURCH

In 1867 I introduced the first purely metaphysical system of healing since the apostolic days. I began by teaching one student Christian Science Mind-healing. From this seed grew the Massachusetts Metaphysical College in Boston, chartered in 1881. No charter was granted for similar purposes after 1883. It is the only College, hitherto, for teaching the pathology of spiritual power, *alias* the Science of Mind-healing.

My husband, Asa G. Eddy, taught two terms in my College. After I gave up teaching, my adopted son, Ebenezer J. Foster-Eddy, a graduate of the Hahneman Medical College of Philadelphia, and who also received a certificate from Dr. W.W. Keen's (allopathic) Philadelphia School of Anatomy and Surgery,—having renounced his material method of practice and embraced the teachings of Christian Science, taught the Primary, Normal, and Obstetric class one term. Gen. Erastus N. Bates taught one Primary class, in 1889, after which I judged it best to close the institution. These students of mine were the only assistant teachers in the College.

The first Christian Scientist Association was organized by myself and six of my students in 1876, on the Centennial Day of our nation's freedom. At a meeting of the Christian Scientist Association, on April 12, 1879, it was voted to organize a church to commemorate the words and works of our Master, a Mind-healing church, without a creed, to be called the Church of Christ, Scientist, the first such church ever organized. The charter for this church was obtained in June, 1879,[5] and during the same month the members, twenty-six in number, extended a call to me to become their pastor. I accepted the call, and was ordained in 1881, though I had preached five years before being ordained.

When I was its pastor, and in the pulpit every Sunday, my church increased in members, and its spiritual growth kept pace with its increasing popularity; but when obliged, because of accumulating work in the College, to preach only occasionally, no student, at that time, was found able to maintain the church in its previous harmony and prosperity.

Examining the situation prayerfully and carefully, noting the church's need, and the predisposing and exciting cause of its condition, I saw that the crisis had come when much time and attention must be given to defend this church from the envy and molestation of other churches, and from the danger to its members which must always lie in Christian warfare. At this juncture I recommended that the church be dissolved. No sooner were my views made known, than the proper measures were adopted to carry them out, the votes passing without a dissenting voice.

---

[5] Steps were taken to promote the Church of Christ, Scientist, in April, May and June; formal organization was accomplished and the charter obtained in August, 1879

This measure was immediately followed by a great revival of mutual love, prosperity, and spiritual power.

The history of that hour holds this true record. Adding to its ranks and influence, this spiritually organized Church of Christ, Scientist, in Boston, still goes on. A new light broke in upon it, and more beautiful became the garments of her who "bringeth good tidings, that publisheth peace."

Despite the prosperity of my church, it was learned that material organization has its value and peril, and that organization is requisite only in the earliest periods in Christian history. After this material form of cohesion and fellowship has accomplished its end, continued organization retards spiritual growth, and should be laid off,—even as the corporeal organization deemed requisite in the first stages of mortal existence is finally laid off, in order to gain spiritual freedom and supremacy.

From careful observation and experience came my clue to the uses and abuses of organization. Therefore, in accord with my special request, followed that noble, unprecedented action of the Christian Scientist Association connected with my College when dissolving that organization,—in forgiving enemies, returning good for evil, in following Jesus' command, "Whosoever shall smite thee on thy right cheek, turn to him the other also." I saw these fruits of Spirit, long-suffering and temperance, fulfil the law of Christ in righteousness. I also saw that Christianity has withstood less the temptation of popularity than of persecution.

"FEED MY SHEEP"

Lines penned when I was pastor of the Church of Christ, Scientist, in Boston.

Shepherd, show me how to go
  O'er the hillside steep,
How to gather, how to sow,—
  How to feed Thy sheep;
I will listen for Thy voice,
  Lest my footsteps stray;
I will follow and rejoice
  All the rugged way.

Thou wilt bind the stubborn will,
  Wound the callous breast,
Make self-righteousness be still,
  Break earth's stupid rest.
Strangers on a barren shore,

Lab'ring long and lone,
We would enter by the door,
  And Thou know'st Thine own.

So, when day grows dark and cold,
  Tear or triumph harms,
Lead Thy lambkins to the fold,
  Take them in Thine arms;
Feed the hungry, heal the heart,
  Till the morning's beam;
White as wool, ere they depart,
  Shepherd, wash them clean.

COLLEGE CLOSED

The apprehension of what has been, and must be, the final outcome of material organization, which wars with Love's spiritual compact, caused me to dread the unprecedented popularity of my College. Students from all over our continent, and from Europe, were flooding the school. At this time there were over three hundred applications from persons desiring to enter the College, and applicants were rapidly increasing. Example had shown the dangers arising from being placed on earthly pinnacles, and Christian Science shuns whatever involves material means for the promotion of spiritual ends.

In view of all this, a meeting was called of the Board of Directors of my College, who, being informed of my intentions, unanimously voted that the school be discontinued.

A Primary class student, richly imbued with the spirit of Christ, is a better healer and teacher than a Normal class student who partakes less of God's love. After having received instructions in a Primary class from me, or a loyal student, and afterwards studied thoroughly Science and Health, a student can enter upon the gospel work of teaching Christian Science, and so fulfil the command of Christ. But before entering this field of labor he must have studied the latest editions of my works, be a good Bible scholar and a consecrated Christian.

The Massachusetts Metaphysical College drew its breath from me, but I was yearning for retirement. The question was, Who else could sustain this institute, under all that was aimed at its vital purpose, the establishment of *genuine* Christian Science healing? My conscientious scruples about diplomas, the recent experience of the church fresh in my thoughts, and the growing conviction that every one should build on his own foundation, subject to the one builder and maker, God,—all these considerations moved me to close my flourishing school, and the following resolutions were passed:—

At a special meeting of the Board of the Metaphysical College

Corporation, Oct. 29, 1889, the following are some of the
resolutions which were presented and passed unanimously:—

WHEREAS, The Massachusetts Metaphysical College,
chartered in January, 1881, for medical purposes, to give
instruction in scientific methods of mental healing on a purely
practical basis, to impart a thorough understanding of
metaphysics, to restore health, hope, and harmony to man,—has
fulfilled its high and noble destiny, and sent to all parts of our
country, and into foreign lands, students instructed in Christian
Science Mind-healing, to meet the demand of the age for something
higher than physic or drugging; and

WHEREAS, The material organization was, in the beginning
in this institution, like the baptism of Jesus, of which he said,
"Suffer it to be so now," though the teaching was a purely
spiritual and scientific impartation of Truth, whose Christly
spirit has led to higher ways, means, and understanding,—the
President, the Rev. Mary B.G. Eddy, at the height of prosperity
in the institution, which yields a large income, is willing to
sacrifice all for the advancement of the world in Truth and Love;
and

WHEREAS, Other institutions for instruction in Christian
Science, which are working out their periods of organization, will
doubtless follow the example of the *Alma Mater* after having
accomplished the worthy purpose for which they were organized, and
the hour has come wherein the great need is for more of the spirit
instead of the letter, and Science and Health is adapted to work
this result; and

WHEREAS, The fundamental principle for growth in
Christian Science is spiritual formation first, last, and always,
while in human growth material organization is first; and

WHEREAS, Mortals must learn to lose their estimate of the
powers that are not ordained of God, and attain the bliss of
loving unselfishly, working patiently, and conquering all that is
unlike Christ and the example he gave; therefore

Resolved, That we thank the State for its charter, which is the
only one ever granted to a *legal college* for teaching the
Science of Mind-healing; that we thank the public for its liberal
patronage. And everlasting gratitude is due to the President, for

her great and noble work, which we believe will prove a healing for the nations, and bring all men to a knowledge of the true God, uniting them in one common brotherhood.

After due deliberation and earnest discussion it was unanimously voted: That as all debts of the corporation have been paid, it is deemed best to dissolve this corporation, and the same is hereby dissolved.

C.A. FRYE, *Clerk*.

When God impelled me to set a price on my instruction in Christian Science Mind-healing, I could think of no financial equivalent for an impartation of a knowledge of that divine power which heals; but I was led to name three hundred dollars as the price for each pupil in one course of lessons at my College,—a startling sum for tuition lasting barely three weeks. This amount greatly troubled me. I shrank from asking it, but was finally led, by a strange providence, to accept this fee.

God has since shown me, in multitudinous ways, the wisdom of this decision; and I beg disinterested people to ask my loyal students if they consider three hundred dollars any real equivalent for my instruction during twelve half-days, or even in half as many lessons. Nevertheless, my list of indigent charity scholars is very large, and I have had as many as seventeen in one class.

Loyal students speak with delight of their pupilage, and of what it has done for them, and for others through them. By loyalty in students I mean this,— allegiance to God, subordination of the human to the divine, steadfast justice, and strict adherence to divine Truth and Love.

I see clearly that students in Christian Science should, at present, continue to organize churches, schools, and associations for the furtherance and unfolding of Truth, and that my necessity is not necessarily theirs; but it was the Father's opportunity for furnishing a new rule of order in divine Science, and the blessings which arose therefrom. Students are not environed with such obstacles as were encountered in the beginning of pioneer work.

In December, 1889, I gave a lot of land in Boston to my student, Mr. Ira O. Knapp of Roslindale,—valued in 1892 at about twenty thousand dollars, and rising in value,—to be appropriated for the erection, and building on the premises thereby conveyed, of a church edifice to be used as a temple for Christian Science worship.

GENERAL ASSOCIATIONS, AND OUR MAGAZINE

For many successive years I have endeavored to find new ways and means for the promotion and expansion of scientific Mind-healing, seeking to broaden its channels and, if possible, to build a hedge round about it that should shelter its perfections from the contaminating influences of those who have a small portion of its letter and less of its spirit. At the same time I have worked to provide a home for every true seeker and honest worker in this vineyard of Truth.

To meet the broader wants of humanity, and provide folds for the sheep that were without shepherds, I suggested to my students, in 1886, the propriety of forming a National Christian Scientist Association. This was immediately done, and delegations from the Christian Scientist Association of the Massachusetts Metaphysical College, and from branch associations in other States, met in general convention at New York City, February 11, 1886.

The first official organ of the Christian Scientist Association was called *Journal of Christian Science*. I started it, April, 1883, as editor and publisher.

To the National Christian Scientist Association, at its meeting in Cleveland, Ohio, June, 1889, I sent a letter, presenting to its loyal members *The Christian Science Journal*, as it was now called, and the funds belonging thereto. This monthly magazine had been made successful and prosperous under difficult circumstances and was designed to bear aloft the standard of genuine Christian Science.

FAITH-CURE

It is often asked, Why are faith-cures sometimes more speedy than some of the cures wrought through Christian Scientists? Because faith is belief, and not understanding; and it is easier to believe, than to understand spiritual Truth. It demands less cross-bearing, self-renunciation, and divine Science to admit the claims of the corporeal senses and appeal to God for relief through a humanized conception of His power, than to deny these claims and learn the divine way,—drinking Jesus' cup, being baptized with his baptism, gaining the end through persecution and purity.

Millions are believing in God, or good, without bearing the fruits of goodness, not having reached its Science. Belief is virtually blindness, when it admits Truth without understanding it. Blind belief cannot say with the apostle, "I know whom I have believed." There is danger in this mental state called belief; for if Truth is admitted, but not understood, it may be lost, and error may enter through this same channel of ignorant belief. The faith-cure has devout followers, whose Christian practice is far in advance of their theory.

The work of healing, in the Science of Mind, is the most sacred and salutary power which can be wielded. My Christian students, impressed with the true sense of the great work before them, enter this strait and narrow path, and work conscientiously.

Let us follow the example of Jesus, the master Metaphysician, and gain sufficient knowledge of error to destroy it with Truth. Evil is not mastered by evil; it can only be overcome with good. This brings out the nothingness of evil and the eternal somethingness, vindicates the divine Principle, and improves the race of Adam.

FOUNDATION-STONES

The following ideas of Deity, antagonized by finite theories, doctrines, and hypotheses, I found to be demonstrable rules in Christian Science, and that we must abide by them.

Whatever diverges from the one divine Mind, or God,—or divides Mind into minds, Spirit into spirits, Soul into souls, and Being into beings,—is a misstatement of the unerring divine Principle of Science, which interrupts the meaning of the omnipotence, omniscience, and omnipresence of Spirit, and is of human instead of divine origin.

War is waged between the evidences of Spirit and the evidences of the five physical senses; and this contest must go on until peace be declared by the final triumph of Spirit in immutable harmony. Divine Science disclaims sin, sickness, and death, on the basis of the omnipotence and omnipresence of God, or divine good.

All consciousness is Mind, and Mind is God. Hence there is but one Mind; and that one is the infinite good, supplying all Mind by the reflection, not the subdivision, of God. Whatever else claims to be mind, or consciousness, is untrue. The sun sends forth light, but not suns; so God reflects Himself, or Mind, but does not subdivide Mind, or good, into minds, good and evil. Divine Science demands mighty wrestlings with mortal beliefs, as we sail into the eternal haven over the unfathomable sea of possibilities.

Neither ancient nor modern philosophy furnishes a scientific basis for the Science of Mind-healing. Plato believed he had a soul, which must be doctored in order to heal his body. This would be like correcting the principle of music for the purpose of destroying discord. Principle is right; it is practice that is wrong. Soul is right; it is the flesh that is evil. Soul is the synonym of Spirit, God; hence there is but one Soul, and that one is infinite. If that pagan philosopher had known that physical sense, not Soul, causes all bodily ailments, his philosophy would have yielded to Science.

Man shines by borrowed light. He reflects God as his Mind, and this reflection is substance,—the substance of good. Matter is substance in error, Spirit is substance in Truth.

Evil, or error, is not Mind; but infinite Mind is sufficient to supply all manifestations of intelligence. The notion of more than one Mind, or Life, is as unsatisfying as it is unscientific. All must be of God, and not our own, separated from Him.

Human systems of philosophy and religion are departures from Christian Science. Mistaking divine Principle for corporeal personality, ingrafting upon one First Cause such opposite effects as good and evil, health and sickness, life and death; making mortality the status and rule of divinity,—such methods can never reach the perfection and demonstration of metaphysical, or Christian Science.

Stating the divine Principle, omnipotence (*omnis potens*), and then departing from this statement and taking the rule of finite matter, with which to work out the problem of infinity or Spirit,—all this is like trying to compensate for the absence of omnipotence by a physical, false, and finite substitute.

With our Master, life was not merely a sense of existence, but an accompanying sense of power that subdued matter and brought to light immortality, insomuch that the people "were astonished at his doctrine: for he taught them as one having authority, and not as the scribes." Life, as defined by Jesus, had no beginning; it was not the result of organization, or infused into matter; it was Spirit.

THE GREAT REVELATION

Christian Science reveals the grand verity, that to believe man has a finite and erring mind, and consequently a mortal mind and soul and life, is error. Scientific terms have no contradictory significations.

In Science, Life is not temporal, but eternal, without beginning or ending. The word *Life* never means that which is the source of death, and of good and evil. Such an inference is unscientific. It is like saying that addition means subtraction in one instance and addition in another, and then applying this rule to a demonstration of the science of numbers; even as mortals apply finite terms to God, in demonstration of infinity. *Life* is a term used to indicate Deity; and every other name for the Supreme Being, if properly employed, has the signification of Life. Whatever errs is mortal, and is the antipodes of Life, or God, and of health and holiness, both in idea and demonstration.

Christian Science reveals Mind, the only living and true God, and all that is made by Him, Mind, as harmonious, immortal, and spiritual: the five material senses define Mind and matter as distinct, but mutually dependent, each on the other, for intelligence and existence. Science defines man as immortal, as coexistent and coeternal with God, as made in His own image and likeness; material sense defines life as something apart from God, beginning and ending, and man as very far from the divine likeness. Science reveals Life as a complete sphere, as eternal, self-existent Mind; material sense defines life as a broken sphere, as organized matter, and mind as something separate from God. Science reveals Spirit as All, averring that there is nothing beside God; material sense says that matter, His antipode, is something besides God. Material sense adds that the divine Spirit created matter, and that matter and evil are as real as Spirit and good.

Christian Science reveals God and His idea as the All and Only. It declares that evil is the absence of good; whereas, good is God ever-present, and therefore evil is unreal and good is all that is real. Christian Science saith to the wave and storm, "Be still," and there is a great calm. Material sense asks, in its ignorance of Science, "When will the raging of the material elements cease?" Science saith to all manner of disease, "Know that God is all-power and all-presence, and there is nothing beside Him;" and the sick are healed. Material sense saith, "Oh, when will my sufferings cease? Where is God? Sickness is something besides Him, which He cannot, or does not, heal."

Christian Science is the only sure basis of harmony. Material sense contradicts Science, for matter and its so-called organizations take no cognizance of the spiritual facts of the universe, or of the real man and God. Christian Science declares that there is but one Truth, Life, Love, but one Spirit, Mind, Soul. Any attempt to divide these arises from the fallibility of sense, from mortal man's ignorance, from enmity to God and divine Science.

Christian Science declares that sickness is a belief, a latent fear, made manifest on the body in different forms of fear or disease. This fear is formed unconsciously in the silent thought, as when you awaken from sleep and feel ill, experiencing the effect of a fear whose existence you do not realize; but if you fall asleep, actually conscious of the truth of Christian Science,—namely, that man's harmony is no more to be invaded than the rhythm of the universe,—you cannot awake in fear or suffering of any sort.

Science saith to fear, "You are the cause of all sickness; but you are a self-constituted falsity,—you are darkness, nothingness. You are without 'hope, and without God in the world.' You do not exist, and have no right to exist, for 'perfect Love casteth out fear.'"

God is everywhere. "There is no speech nor language, where their voice is not heard;" and this voice is Truth that destroys error and Love that casts out fear.

Christian Science reveals the fact that, if suffering exists, it is in the mortal mind only, for matter has no sensation and cannot suffer.

If you rule out every sense of disease and suffering from mortal mind, it cannot be found in the body.

Posterity will have the right to demand that Christian Science be stated and demonstrated in its godliness and grandeur,—that however little be taught or learned, that little shall be right. Let there be milk for babes, but let not the milk be adulterated. Unless this method be pursued, the Science of Christian healing will again be lost, and human suffering will increase.

Test Christian Science by its effect on society, and you will find that the views here set forth—as to the illusion of sin, sickness, and death—bring forth better fruits of health, righteousness, and Life, than *a belief in their reality has ever done.* A demonstration of the *unreality* of evil destroys evil.

SIN, SINNER, AND ECCLESIASTICISM

Why do Christian Scientists say God and His idea are the only realities, and then insist on the need of healing sickness and sin? Because Christian Science heals sin as it heals sickness, by establishing the recognition that God *is All*, and there is none beside Him,—that all is good, and there is in reality no evil, neither sickness nor sin. We attack the sinner's belief in the pleasure of sin, *alias* the reality of sin, which makes him a sinner, in order to destroy this belief and save him from sin; and we attack the belief of the sick in the reality of sickness, in order to heal them. When we deny the authority of sin, we begin to sap it; for this denunciation must precede its destruction.

God is good, hence goodness is something, for it represents God, the Life of man. Its opposite, nothing, named *evil*, is nothing but a conspiracy against man's Life and goodness. Do you not feel bound to expose this conspiracy, and so to save man from it? Whosoever covers iniquity becomes accessory to it. Sin, as a claim, is more dangerous than sickness, more subtle, more difficult to heal.

St. Augustine once said, "The devil is but the ape of God." Sin is worse than sickness; but recollect that it encourages sin to say, "There is no sin," and leave the subject there.

Sin ultimates in sinner, and in this sense they are one. You cannot separate sin from the sinner, nor the sinner from his sin. The sin is the sinner, and *vice versa*, for such is the unity of evil; and together both sinner and sin will be destroyed by the supremacy of good. This, however, does not annihilate man, for to efface sin, *alias* the sinner, brings to light, makes apparent, the real man, even God's "image and likeness." Need it be said that any opposite theory is heterodox to divine Science, which teaches that good is equally *one* and *all*, even as the opposite claim of evil is one.

In Christian Science the fact is made obvious that the sinner and the sin are alike simply nothingness; and this view is supported by the Scripture, where the Psalmist saith: "He shall go to the generation of his fathers; they shall never see light. Man that is in honor, and understandeth not, is like the beasts that perish." God's ways and works and thoughts have never changed, either in Principle or practice.

Since there is in belief an illusion termed sin, which must be met and mastered, we classify sin, sickness, and death as illusions. They are supposititious claims of error; and error being a false claim, they are no claims at all. It is scientific to abide in conscious harmony, in health-giving, deathless Truth and Love. To do this, mortals must first open their eyes to all the illusive forms, methods, and subtlety of error, in order that the illusion, error, may be destroyed; if this is not done, mortals will become the victims of error.

If evangelical churches refuse fellowship with the Church of Christ, Scientist, or with Christian Science, they must rest their opinions of Truth and Love on the evidences of the physical senses, rather than on the teaching and practice of Jesus, or the works of the Spirit.

Ritualism and dogma lead to self-righteousness and bigotry, which freeze out the spiritual element. Pharisaism killeth; Spirit giveth Life. The odors of persecution, tobacco, and alcohol are not the sweet-smelling savor of Truth and Love. Feasting the senses, gratification of appetite and passion, have no warrant in the gospel or the Decalogue. Mortals must take up the cross if they would follow Christ, and worship the Father "in spirit and in truth."

The Jewish religion was not spiritual; hence Jesus denounced it. If the religion of to-day is constituted of such elements as of old ruled Christ out of the synagogues, it will continue to avoid whatever follows the example of our Lord and prefers Christ to creed. Christian Science is the pure evangelic truth. It accords with the trend and tenor of Christ's teaching and example, while it demonstrates the power of Christ as taught in the four Gospels. Truth, casting out evils and healing the sick; Love, fulfilling the law and keeping man unspotted from the world,—these practical manifestations of Christianity constitute the only evangelism, and they need no creed.

As well expect to determine, without a telescope, the magnitude and distance of the stars, as to expect to obtain health, harmony, and holiness through an unspiritual and unhealing religion. Christianity reveals God as ever-present Truth and Love, to be utilized in healing the sick, in casting out error, in raising the dead.

Christian Science gives vitality to religion, which is no longer buried in materiality. It raises men from a material sense into the spiritual understanding and scientific demonstration of God.

THE HUMAN CONCEPT

Sin existed as a false claim before the human concept of sin was formed; hence one's concept of error is not the whole of error. The human thought does not constitute sin, but *vice versa*, sin constitutes the human or physical concept.

Sin is both concrete and abstract. Sin was, and *is*, the lying supposition that life, substance, and intelligence are both material and spiritual, and yet are separate from God. The first iniquitous manifestation of sin was a finity. The finite was self-arrayed against the infinite, the mortal against immortality, and a sinner was the antipode of God.

Silencing self, *alias* rising above corporeal personality, is what reforms the sinner and destroys sin. In the ratio that the testimony of material personal sense ceases, sin diminishes, until the false claim called sin is finally lost for lack of witness.

The sinner created neither himself nor sin, but sin created the sinner; that is, error made its man mortal, and this mortal was the image and likeness of evil, not of good. Therefore the lie was, and *is*, collective as well as individual. It was in no way contingent on Adam's thought, but supposititiously self-created. In the words of our Master, it, the "devil" (*alias* evil), "was a liar, and the father of it."

This mortal material concept was never a creator, although as a serpent it claimed to originate in the name of "the Lord," or good,—original evil; second, in the name of human concept, it claimed to beget the offspring of evil, *alias* an evil offspring. However, the human concept never was, neither indeed can be, the father of man. Even the spiritual idea, or ideal man, is not a parent, though he reflects the infinity of good. The great difference between these opposites is, that the human material concept is *unreal*, and the divine concept or idea is spiritually real. One is false, while the other is true. One is temporal, but the other is eternal.

Our Master instructed his students to "call no man your father upon the earth: for one is your Father, which is in heaven." (Matt. xxiii. 9.)

Science and Health, the textbook of Christian Science, treats of the human concept, and the transference of thought, as follows:—

"How can matter originate or transmit mind? We answer that it cannot. Darkness and doubt encompass thought, so long as it bases creation on materiality" (p. 551).

"In reality there is no *mortal* mind, and consequently no transference of mortal thought and will-power. Life and being are of God. In Christian Science, man can do no harm, for scientific thoughts are true thoughts, passing from God to man" (pp. 103, 104).

"Man is the offspring of Spirit. The beautiful, good, and pure constitute his ancestry. His origin is not, like that of mortals, in brute instinct, nor does he pass through material conditions prior to reaching intelligence. Spirit is his primitive and ultimate source of being; God is his Father, and Life is the law of his being" (p. 63).

"The parent of all human discord was the Adam-dream, the deep sleep, in which originated the delusion that life and intelligence proceeded from and passed into matter. This pantheistic error, or so-called *serpent*, insists still upon the opposite of Truth, saying, 'Ye shall be as gods;' that is, I will make error as real and eternal as Truth.... 'I will put spirit into what I call matter, and matter shall seem to have life as much as God, Spirit, who *is* the only Life.' This error has proved itself to be error. Its life is found to be not Life, but only a transient, false sense of an existence which ends in death" (pp. 306, 307).

"When will the error of believing that there is life in matter,
and that sin, sickness, and death are creations of God, be
unmasked? When will it be understood that matter has no
intelligence, life, nor sensation, and that the opposite belief is
the prolific source of all suffering? God created all through
Mind, and made all perfect and eternal. Where then is the
necessity for recreation or procreation?" (p. 205).

"Above error's awful din, blackness, and chaos, the voice of Truth
still calls: 'Adam, where art thou? Consciousness, where art thou?
Art thou dwelling in the belief that mind is in matter, and that
evil is mind, or art thou in the living faith that there is and
can be but one God, and keeping His commandment?'" (pp. 307,
308). "Mortal mind inverts the true likeness, and confers animal
names and natures upon its own misconceptions. Ignorant of the
origin and operations of mortal mind,—that is, ignorant of
itself,—this so-called mind puts forth its own qualities, and
claims God as their author;... usurps the deific prerogatives and
is an attempted infringement on infinity" (pp. 512, 513).

We do not question the authenticity of the Scriptural narrative of the Virgin-
mother and Bethlehem babe, and the Messianic mission of Christ Jesus; but in
our time no Christian Scientist will give chimerical wings to his imagination, or
advance speculative theories as to the recurrence of such events.

No person can take the individual place of the Virgin Mary. No person can
compass or fulfil the individual mission of Jesus of Nazareth. No person can
take the place of the author of Science and Health, the Discoverer and Founder
of Christian Science. Each individual must fill his own niche in time and eternity.

The second appearing of Jesus is, unquestionably, the spiritual advent of the
advancing idea of God, as in Christian Science.

And the scientific ultimate of this God-idea must be, will be, forever
individual, incorporeal, and infinite, even the reflection, "image and likeness," of
the infinite God.

The right teacher of Christian Science lives the truth he teaches. Preeminent
among men, he virtually stands at the head of all sanitary, civil, moral, and
religious reform. Such a post of duty, unpierced by vanity, exalts a mortal
beyond human praise, or monuments which weigh dust, and humbles him with
the tax it raises on calamity to open the gates of heaven. It is not the forager on
others' wisdom that God thus crowns, but he who is obedient to the divine
command, "Render to Cæsar the things that are Cæsar's, and to God the things
that are God's."

Great temptations beset an ignorant or an unprincipled mind-practice in
opposition to the straight and narrow path of Christian Science. Promiscuous
mental treatment, without the consent or knowledge of the individual treated, is
an error of much magnitude. People unaware of the indications of mental

treatment, know not what is affecting them, and thus may be robbed of their individual rights,—freedom of choice and self-government. Who is willing to be subjected to such an influence? Ask the unbridled mind-manipulator if he would consent to this; and if not, then he is knowingly transgressing Christ's command. He who secretly manipulates mind without the permission of man or God, is not dealing justly and loving mercy, according to pure and undefiled religion.

Sinister and selfish motives entering into mental practice are dangerous incentives; they proceed from false convictions and a fatal ignorance. These are the tares growing side by side with the wheat, that must be recognized, and uprooted, before the wheat can be garnered and Christian Science demonstrated.

Secret mental efforts to obtain help from one who is unaware of this attempt, demoralizes the person who does this, the same as other forms of stealing, and will end in destroying health and morals.

In the practice of Christian Science one cannot impart a mental influence that hazards another's happiness, nor interfere with the rights of the individual. To disregard the welfare of others is contrary to the law of God; therefore it deteriorates one's ability to do good, to benefit himself and mankind.

The Psalmist vividly portrays the result of secret faults, presumptuous sins, and self-deception, in these words: "How are they brought into desolation, as in a moment! They are utterly consumed with terrors."

PERSONALITY

The immortal man being spiritual, individual, and eternal, his mortal opposite must be material, corporeal, and temporal. Physical personality is finite; but God is infinite. He is without materiality, without finiteness of form or Mind.

Limitations are put off in proportion as the fleshly nature disappears and man is found in the reflection of Spirit.

This great fact leads into profound depths. The material human concept grew beautifully less as I floated into more spiritual latitudes and purer realms of thought.

From that hour personal corporeality became less to me than it is to people who fail to appreciate individual character. I endeavored to lift thought above physical personality, or selfhood in matter, to man's spiritual individuality in God,—in the true Mind, where sensible evil is lost in supersensible good. This is the only way whereby the false personality is laid off.

He who clings to personality, or perpetually warns you of "personality," wrongs it, or terrifies people over it, and is the sure victim of his own corporeality. Constantly to scrutinize physical personality, or accuse people of being unduly personal, is like the sick talking sickness. Such errancy betrays a violent and egotistical personality, increases one's sense of corporeality, and begets a fear of the senses and a perpetually egotistical sensibility.

He who does this is ignorant of the meaning of the word *personality*, and defines it by his own *corpus sine pectore* (soulless body), and fails to distinguish the individual, or real man from the false sense of corporeality, or egotistic self.

My own corporeal personality afflicteth me not wittingly; for I desire never to think of it, and it cannot think of me.

PLAGIARISM

The various forms of book-borrowing without credit spring from this ill-concealed question in mortal mind, Who shall be greatest? This error violates the law given by Moses, it tramples upon Jesus' Sermon on the Mount, it does violence to the ethics of Christian Science.

Why withhold my name, while appropriating my language and ideas, but give credit when citing from the works of other authors?

Life and its ideals are inseparable, and one's writings on ethics, and demonstration of Truth, are not, cannot be, understood or taught by those who persistently misunderstand or misrepresent the author. Jesus said, "For there is no man which shall do a miracle in my name, that can lightly speak evil of me."

If one's spiritual ideal is comprehended and loved, the borrower from it is embraced in the author's own mental mood, and is therefore *honest*. The Science of Mind excludes opposites, and rests on unity.

It is proverbial that dishonesty retards spiritual growth and strikes at the heart of Truth. If a student at Harvard College has studied a textbook written by his teacher, is he entitled, when he leaves the University, to write out as his own the substance of this textbook? There is no warrant in common law and no permission in the gospel for plagiarizing an author's ideas and their words. Christian Science is not copyrighted; nor would protection by copyright be requisite, if mortals obeyed God's law of *manright*. A student can write voluminous works on Science without trespassing, if he writes honestly, and he cannot dishonestly compose *Christian Science*. The Bible is not stolen, though it is cited, and quoted deferentially.

Thoughts touched with the Spirit and Word of Christian Science gravitate naturally toward Truth. Therefore the mind to which this Science was revealed must have risen to the altitude which perceived a light beyond what others saw.

The spiritually minded meet on the stairs which lead up to spiritual love. This affection, so far from being personal worship, fulfils the law of Love which Paul enjoined upon the Galatians. This is the Mind "which was also in Christ Jesus," and knows no material limitations. It is the unity of good and bond of perfectness. This just affection serves to constitute the Mind-healer a wonder-worker,—as of old, on the Pentecost Day, when the disciples were of one accord.

He who gains the God-crowned summit of Christian Science never abuses the corporeal personality, but uplifts it. He thinks of every one in his real quality, and sees each mortal in an impersonal depict.

I have long remained silent on a growing evil in plagiarism; but if I do not insist upon the strictest observance of moral law and order in Christian Scientists, I become responsible, as a teacher, for laxity in discipline and lawlessness in literature. Pope was right in saying, "An honest man's the noblest work of God;" and Ingersoll's repartee has its moral: "An honest God's the noblest work of man."

ADMONITION

The neophyte in Christian Science acts like a diseased physique,—being too fast or too slow. He is inclined to do either too much or too little. In healing and teaching the student has not yet achieved the entire wisdom of Mind-practice. The textual explanation of this practice is complete in Science and Health; and scientific practice makes perfect, for it is governed by its Principle, and not by human opinions; but carnal and sinister motives, entering into this practice, will prevent the demonstration of Christian Science.

I recommend students not to read so-called scientific works, antagonistic to Christian Science, which advocate materialistic systems; because such works and words becloud the right sense of metaphysical Science.

The rules of Mind-healing are wholly Christlike and spiritual. Therefore the adoption of a worldly policy or a resort to subterfuge in the statement of the Science of Mind-healing, or any name given to it other than Christian Science, or an attempt to demonstrate the facts of this Science other than is stated in Science and Health—is a departure from the Science of Mind-healing. To becloud mortals, or for yourself to hide from God, is to conspire against the blessings otherwise conferred, against your own success and final happiness, against the progress of the human race as well as against *honest* metaphysical theory and practice.

Not by the hearing of the ear is spiritual truth learned and loved; nor cometh this apprehension from the experiences of others. We glean spiritual harvests from our own material losses. In this consuming heat false images are effaced from the canvas of mortal mind; and thus does the material pigment beneath fade into invisibility.

The signs for the wayfarer in divine Science lie in meekness, in unselfish motives and acts, in shuffling off scholastic rhetoric, in ridding the thought of effete doctrines, in the purification of the affections and desires.

Dishonesty, envy, and mad ambition are "lusts of the flesh," which uproot the germs of growth in Science and leave the inscrutable problem of being unsolved. Through the channels of material sense, of worldly policy, pomp, and pride, cometh no success in Truth. If beset with misguided emotions, we shall be stranded on the quicksands of worldly commotion, and practically come short of the wisdom requisite for teaching and demonstrating the victory over self and sin.

Be temperate in thought, word, and deed. Meekness and temperance are the jewels of Love, set in wisdom. Restrain untempered zeal. "Learn to labor and to wait." Of old the children of Israel were saved by patient waiting.

"The kingdom of heaven suffereth violence, and the violent take it by force!" said Jesus. Therefore are its spiritual gates not captured, nor its golden streets invaded.

We recognize this kingdom, the reign of harmony within us, by an unselfish affection or love, for this is the pledge of divine good and the insignia of heaven. This also is proverbial, that though eternal justice be graciously gentle, yet it may seem severe.

For whom the Lord loveth He chasteneth,
And scourgeth every son whom He receiveth.

As the poets in different languages have expressed it:—

Though the mills of God grind slowly,
  Yet they grind exceeding small;
Though with patience He stands waiting,
  With exactness grinds He all.

Though the divine rebuke is effectual to the pulling down of sin's strongholds, it may stir the human heart to resist Truth, before this heart becomes obediently receptive of the heavenly discipline. If the Christian Scientist recognize the mingled sternness and gentleness which permeate justice and Love, he will not scorn the timely reproof, but will so absorb it that this warning will be within him a spring, welling up into unceasing spiritual rise and progress. Patience and obedience win the golden scholarship of experimental tuition.

The kindly shepherd of the East carries his lambs in his arms to the sheepcot, but the older sheep pass into the fold under his compelling rod. He who sees the door and turns away from it, is guilty, while innocence strayeth yearningly.

There are no greater miracles known to earth than perfection and an unbroken friendship. We love our friends, but ofttimes we lose them in proportion to our affection. The sacrifices made for others are not infrequently met by envy, ingratitude, and enmity, which smite the heart and threaten to paralyze its beneficence. The unavailing tear is shed both for the living and the dead.

Nothing except sin, in the students themselves, can separate them from me. Therefore we should guard thought and action, keeping them in accord with Christ, and our friendship will surely continue.

The letter of the law of God, separated from its spirit, tends to demoralize mortals, and must be corrected by a diviner sense of liberty and light. The spirit of Truth extinguishes false thinking, feeling, and acting; and falsity must thus decay, ere spiritual sense, affectional consciousness, and genuine goodness become so apparent as to be well understood.

After the supreme advent of Truth in the heart, there comes an overwhelming sense of error's vacuity, of the blunders which arise from wrong apprehension. The enlightened heart loathes error, and casts it aside; or else that heart is consciously untrue to the light, faithless to itself and to others, and so sinks into deeper darkness. Said Jesus: "If the light that is in thee be darkness, how great is that darkness!" and Shakespeare puts this pious counsel into a father's mouth:—

> This above all: To thine own self be true;
> And it must follow, as the night the day,
> Thou canst not then be false to any man.

A realization of the shifting scenes of human happiness, and of the frailty of mortal anticipations,—such as first led me to the feet of Christian Science,— seems to be requisite at every stage of advancement. Though our first lessons are changed, modified, broadened, yet their core is constantly renewed; as the law of the chord remains unchanged, whether we are dealing with a simple Latour exercise or with the vast Wagner Trilogy.

A general rule is, that my students should not allow their movements to be controlled by other students, even if they are teachers and practitioners of the same blessed faith. The exception to this rule should be very rare.

The widest power and strongest growth have always been attained by those loyal students who rest on divine Principle for guidance, not on themselves; and who locate permanently in one section, and adhere to the orderly methods herein delineated.

At this period my students should locate in large cities, in order to do the greatest good to the greatest number, and therein abide. The population of our principal cities is ample to supply many practitioners, teachers, and preachers with work. This fact interferes in no way with the prosperity of each worker; rather does it represent an accumulation of power on his side which promotes the ease and welfare of the workers. Their liberated capacities of mind enable Christian Scientists to consummate much good or else evil; therefore their examples either excel or fall short of other religionists; and they must be found dwelling together in harmony, if even they compete with ecclesiastical fellowship and friendship.

It is often asked which revision of Science and Health is the best. The arrangement of my last revision, in 1890, makes the subject-matter clearer than any previous edition, and it is therefore better adapted to spiritualize thought and elucidate scientific healing and teaching. It has already been proven that this volume is accomplishing the divine purpose to a remarkable degree. The wise Christian Scientist will commend students and patients to the teachings of this book, and the healing efficacy thereof, rather than try to centre their interest on himself.

Students whom I have taught are seldom benefited by the teachings of other students, for scientific foundations are already laid in their minds which ought not to be tampered with. Also, they are prepared to receive the infinite instructions afforded by the Bible and my books, which mislead no one and are their best guides.

The student may mistake in his conception of Truth, and this error, in an honest heart, is sure to be corrected. But if he misinterprets the text to his pupils, and communicates, even unintentionally, his misconception of Truth, thereafter he will find it more difficult to rekindle his own light or to enlighten them. Hence, as a rule, the student should explain only Recapitulation, the chapter for the class-room, and leave Science and Health to God's daily interpretation.

Christian Scientists should take their textbook into the schoolroom the same as other teachers; they should ask questions from it, and be answered according to it,—occasionally reading aloud from the book to corroborate what they teach. It is also highly important that their pupils study each lesson before the recitation.

That these essential points are ever omitted, is anomalous, when we consider the necessity of thoroughly understanding Science, and the present liability of deviating from absolute Christian Science.

Centuries will intervene before the statement of the inexhaustible topics of Science and Health is sufficiently understood to be fully demonstrated.

The teacher himself should continue to study this textbook, and to spiritualize his own thoughts and human life from this open fount of Truth and Love.

He who sees clearly and enlightens other minds most readily, keeps his own lamp trimmed and burning. Throughout his entire explanations he strictly adheres to the teachings in the chapter on Recapitulation. When closing the class, each member should own a copy of Science and Health, and continue to study and assimilate this inexhaustible subject—Christian Science.

The opinions of men cannot be substituted for God's revelation. In times past, arrogant pride, in attempting to steady the ark of Truth, obscured even the power and glory of the Scriptures,—to which Science and Health is the Key.

That teacher does most for his students who divests himself most of pride and self, and by reason thereof is able to empty his students' minds of error, that they may be filled with Truth. Thus doing, posterity will call him blessed, and the tired tongue of history be enriched.

The less the teacher personally controls other minds, and the more he trusts them to the divine Truth and Love, the better it will be for both teacher and student.

A teacher should take charge only of his own pupils and patients, and of those who voluntarily place themselves under his direction; he should avoid leaving his own regular institute or place of labor, or expending his labor where there are other teachers who should be specially responsible for doing their own work well.

Teachers of Christian Science will find it advisable to band together their students into associations, to continue the organization of churches, and at present they can employ any other organic operative method that may commend itself as useful to the Cause and beneficial to mankind.

Of this also rest assured, that books and teaching are but a ladder let down from the heaven of Truth and Love, upon which angelic thoughts ascend and descend, bearing on their pinions of light the Christ-spirit.

Guard yourselves against the subtly hidden suggestion that the Son of man will be glorified, or humanity benefited, by any deviation from the order prescribed by supernal grace. Seek to occupy no position whereto you do not feel that God ordains you. Never forsake your post without due deliberation and light, but always wait for God's finger to point the way. The loyal Christian Scientist is incapable alike of abusing the practice of Mind-healing or of healing on a material basis.

The tempter is vigilant, awaiting only an opportunity to divide the ranks of Christian Science and scatter the sheep abroad; but "if God be for us, who can be against us?" The Cause, *our* Cause, is highly prosperous, rapidly spreading over the globe; and the morrow will crown the effort of to-day with a diadem of gems from the New Jerusalem.

EXEMPLIFICATION

To energize wholesome spiritual warfare, to rebuke vainglory, to offset boastful emptiness, to crown patient toil, and rejoice in the spirit and power of Christian Science, we must ourselves be true. There is but one way of *doing* good, and that is to *do* it! There is but one way of *being* good, and that is to *be* good!

Art thou still unacquainted with thyself? Then be introduced to this self. "Know thyself!" as said the classic Grecian motto. Note well the falsity of this mortal self! Behold its vileness, and remember this poverty-stricken "stranger that is within thy gates." Cleanse every stain from this wanderer's soiled garments, wipe the dust from his feet and the tears from his eyes, that you may behold the real man, the fellow-saint of a holy household. There should be no blot on the escutcheon of our Christliness when we offer our gift upon the altar.

A student desiring growth in the knowledge of Truth, can and will obtain it by taking up his cross and following Truth. If he does this not, and another one undertakes to carry his burden and do his work, the duty will *not be accomplished*. No one can save himself without God's help, and God will help each man who performs his own part. After this manner and in no other way is every man cared for and blessed. To the unwise helper our Master said, "Follow me; and let the dead bury their dead."

The poet's line, "Order is heaven's first law," is so eternally true, so axiomatic, that it has become a truism; and its wisdom is as obvious in religion and scholarship as in astronomy or mathematics.

Experience has taught me that the rules of Christian Science can be far more thoroughly and readily acquired by regularly settled and systematic workers, than by unsettled and spasmodic efforts. Genuine Christian Scientists are, or should be, the most systematic and law-abiding people on earth, because their religion demands implicit adherence to fixed rules, in the orderly demonstration thereof. Let some of these rules be here stated.

First: Christian Scientists are to "heal the sick" as the Master commanded.

In so doing they must follow the divine order as prescribed by Jesus,— never, in any way, to trespass upon the rights of their neighbors, but to obey the celestial injunction, "Whatsoever ye would that men should do to you, do ye even so to them."

In this orderly, scientific dispensation healers become a law unto themselves. They feel their own burdens less, and can therefore bear the weight of others' burdens, since it is only through the lens of their unselfishness that the sunshine of Truth beams with such efficacy as to dissolve error.

It is already understood that Christian Scientists will not receive a patient who is under the care of a regular physician, until he has done with the case and different aid is sought. The same courtesy should be observed in the professional intercourse of Christian Science healers with one another.

Second: Another command of the Christ, his prime command, was that his followers should "raise the dead." He lifted his own body from the sepulchre. In him, Truth called the physical man from the tomb to health, and the so-called dead forthwith emerged into a higher manifestation of Life.

The spiritual significance of this command, "Raise the dead," most concerns mankind. It implies such an elevation of the understanding as will enable thought to apprehend the living beauty of Love, its practicality, its divine energies, its health-giving and life-bestowing qualities,—yea, its power to demonstrate immortality. This end Jesus achieved, both by example and precept.

Third: This leads inevitably to a consideration of another part of Christian Science work,—a part which concerns us intimately,—preaching the gospel.

This evangelistic duty should not be so warped as to signify that we must or may go, uninvited, to work in other vineyards than our own. One would, or should, blush to enter unasked another's pulpit, and preach without the consent of the stated occupant of that pulpit. The Lord's command means this, that we should adopt the spirit of the Saviour's ministry, and abide in such a spiritual attitude as will draw men unto us. Itinerancy should not be allowed to clip the wings of divine Science. Mind demonstrates omnipresence and omnipotence, but Mind revolves on a spiritual axis, and its power is displayed and its presence felt in eternal stillness and immovable Love. The divine potency of this spiritual mode of Mind, and the hindrance opposed to it by material motion, is proven beyond a doubt in the practice of Mind-healing.

In those days preaching and teaching were substantially one. There was no church preaching, in the modern sense of the term. Men assembled in the one temple (at Jerusalem) for sacrificial ceremonies, not for sermons. Into the synagogues, scattered about in cities and villages, they went for liturgical worship, and instruction in the Mosaic law. If one worshipper preached to the others, he did so informally, and because he was bidden to this privileged duty at that particular moment. It was the custom to pay this hortatory compliment to a stranger, or to a member who had been away from the neighborhood; as Jesus was once asked to exhort, when he had been some time absent from Nazareth but once again entered the synagogue which he had frequented in childhood.

Jesus' method was to instruct his own students; and he watched and guarded them unto the end, even according to his promise, "Lo, I am with you alway!" Nowhere in the four Gospels will Christian Scientists find any precedent for employing another student to take charge of their students, or for neglecting their own students, in order to enlarge their sphere of action.

Above all, trespass not intentionally upon other people's thoughts, by endeavoring to influence other minds to any action not first made known to them or sought by them. Corporeal and selfish influence is human, fallible, and temporary; but incorporeal impulsion is divine, infallible, and eternal. The student should be most careful not to thrust aside Science, and shade God's window which lets in light, or seek to stand in God's stead.

Does the faithful shepherd forsake the lambs,—retaining his salary for tending the home flock while he is serving another fold? There is no evidence to show that Jesus ever entered the towns whither he sent his disciples; no evidence that he there taught a few hungry ones, and then left them to starve or to stray. To these selected ones (like "the elect lady" to whom St. John addressed one of his epistles) he gave personal instruction, and gave in plain words, until they were able to fulfil his behest and depart on their united pilgrimages. This he did, even though one of the twelve whom he kept near himself betrayed him, and others forsook him.

The true mother never willingly neglects her children in their early and sacred hours, consigning them to the care of nurse or stranger. Who can feel and comprehend the needs of her babe like the ardent mother? What other heart yearns with her solicitude, endures with her patience, waits with her hope, and labors with her love, to promote the welfare and happiness of her children? Thus must the Mother in Israel give all her hours to those first sacred tasks, till her children can walk steadfastly in wisdom's ways.

One of my students wrote to me: "I believe the proper thing for us to do is to follow, as nearly as we can, in the path you have pursued!" It is gladdening to find, in such a student, one of the children of light. It is safe to leave with God the government of man. He appoints and He anoints His Truth-bearers, and God is their sure defense and refuge.

The parable of "the prodigal son" is rightly called "the pearl of parables," and our Master's greatest utterance may well be called "the diamond sermon." No purer and more exalted teachings ever fell upon human ears than those contained in what is commonly known as the Sermon on the Mount,—though this name has been given it by compilers and translators of the Bible, and not by the Master himself or by the Scripture authors. Indeed, this title really indicates more the Master's mood, than the material locality.

Where did Jesus deliver this great lesson—or, rather, this series of great lessons—on humanity and divinity? On a hillside, near the sloping shores of the Lake of Galilee, where he spake primarily to his immediate disciples.

In this simplicity, and with such fidelity, we see Jesus ministering to the spiritual needs of all who placed themselves under his care, always leading them into the divine order, under the sway of his own perfect understanding. His power over others was spiritual, not corporeal. To the students whom he had chosen, his immortal teaching was the bread of Life. When *he* was with them, a fishing-boat became a sanctuary, and the solitude was peopled with holy messages from the All-Father. The grove became his class-room, and nature's haunts were the Messiah's university.

What has this hillside priest, this seaside teacher, done for the human race? Ask, rather, what has he *not* done. His holy humility, unworldliness, and self-abandonment wrought infinite results. The method of his religion was not too simple to be sublime, nor was his power so exalted as to be unavailable for the needs of suffering mortals, whose wounds he healed by Truth and Love.

His order of ministration was "first the blade, then the ear, after that the full corn in the ear." May we unloose the latchets of his Christliness, inherit his legacy of love, and reach the fruition of his promise: "If ye abide in me, and my words abide in you, ye shall ask what ye will, and it shall be done unto you."

WAYMARKS

In the first century of the Christian era Jesus went about doing good. The evangelists of those days wandered about. Christ, or the spiritual idea, appeared to human consciousness as the man Jesus. At the present epoch the human concept of Christ is based on the incorporeal divine Principle of man, and Science has elevated this idea and established its rules in consonance with their Principle. Hear this saying of our Master, "And I, if I be lifted up from the earth, will draw all men unto me."

The ideal of God is no longer impersonated as a waif or wanderer; and Truth is not fragmentary, disconnected, unsystematic, but concentrated and immovably fixed in Principle. The best spiritual type of Christly method for uplifting human thought and imparting divine Truth, is stationary power, stillness, and strength; and when this spiritual ideal is made our own, it becomes the model for human action.

St. Paul said to the Athenians, "For in Him we live, and move, and have our being." This statement is in substance identical with my own: "There is no life, truth, substance, nor intelligence in matter." It is quite clear that as yet this grandest verity has not been fully demonstrated, but it is nevertheless true. If Christian Science reiterates St. Paul's teaching, we, as Christian Scientists, should give to the world convincing proof of the validity of this scientific statement of being. Having perceived, in advance of others, this scientific fact, we owe to ourselves and to the world a struggle for its demonstration.

At some period and in some way the conclusion must be met that whatsoever seems true, and yet contradicts divine Science and St. Paul's text, must be and is false; and that whatsoever seems to be good, and yet errs, though acknowledging the true way, is really evil.

As dross is separated from gold, so Christ's baptism of fire, his purification through suffering, consumes whatsoever is of sin. Therefore this purgation of divine mercy, destroying all error, leaves no flesh, no matter, to the mental consciousness.

When all fleshly belief is annihilated, and every spot and blemish on the disk of consciousness is removed, then, and not till then, will immortal Truth be found true, and scientific teaching, preaching, and practice be essentially one. "Happy is he that condemneth not himself in that thing which he alloweth ... for whatsoever is not of faith is sin." (Romans xiv. 22, 23.)

There is no "lo here! or lo there!" in divine Science; its manifestation must be "the same yesterday, and to-day, and forever," since Science is eternally one, and unchanging, in Principle, rule, and demonstration.

I am persuaded that only by the modesty and distinguishing affection illustrated in Jesus' career, can Christian Scientists aid the establishment of Christ's kingdom on the earth. In the first century of the Christian era Jesus' teachings bore much fruit, and the Father was glorified therein. In this period and the forthcoming centuries, watered by dews of divine Science, this "tree of life" will blossom into greater freedom, and its leaves will be "for the healing of the nations."

Ask God to give thee skill
  In comfort's art:
That thou may'st consecrated be
  And set apart
Unto a life of sympathy.
For heavy is the weight of ill
  In every heart;
And comforters are needed much
  Of Christlike touch.

—A.E. HAMILTON.

RUDIMENTAL DIVINE SCIENCE

By MARY BAKER EDDY

Published by The Trustees under the Will of Mary
Baker G. Eddy

1891, 1908

THIS LITTLE BOOK IS TENDERLY AND RESPECTFULLY
DEDICATED TO ALL LOYAL
 STUDENTS, WORKING AND WAITING FOR THE ESTABLISHMENT
OF THE SCIENCE OF
 MIND-HEALING
                    MARY BAKER EDDY

CONTENTS

DEFINITION OF CHRISTIAN SCIENCE

How would you define Christian Science?

As the law of God, the law of good, interpreting and demonstrating the divine Principle and rule of universal harmony.

What is the Principle of Christian Science?

It is God, the Supreme Being, infinite and immortal Mind, the Soul of man and the universe. It is our Father which is in heaven. It is substance, Spirit, Life, Truth, and Love,—these are the deific Principle.

Do you mean by this that God is a person?

The word *person* affords a large margin for misapprehension, as well as definition. In French the equivalent word is *personne*. In Spanish, Italian, and Latin, it is *persona*. The Latin verb *personare* is compounded of the prefix *per* (through) and *sonare* (to sound).

In law, Blackstone applies the word *personal* to *bodily presence*, in distinction from one's appearance (in court, for example) by deputy or proxy.

Other definitions of *person*, as given by Webster, are "a living soul; a self-conscious being; a moral agent; especially, a living human being, a corporeal man, woman, or child; an individual of the human race." He adds, that among Trinitarian Christians the word stands for one of the three subjects, or agents, constituting the Godhead.

In Christian Science we learn that God is definitely individual, and not a *person*, as that word is used by the best authorities, if our lexicographers are right in defining *person* as especially a finite *human being*; but God is personal, if by *person* is meant infinite Spirit.

We do not conceive rightly of God, if we think of Him as less than infinite. The human person is finite; and therefore I prefer to retain the proper sense of Deity by using the phrase *an individual* God, rather than *a personal* God; for there is and can be but one infinite individual Spirit, whom mortals have named God.

Science defines the individuality of God as supreme good, Life, Truth, Love. This term enlarges our sense of Deity, takes away the trammels assigned to God by finite thought, and introduces us to higher definitions.

Is healing the sick the whole of Science?

Healing physical sickness is the smallest part of Christian Science. It is only the bugle-call to thought and action, in the higher range of infinite goodness. The emphatic purpose of Christian Science is the healing of sin; and this task, sometimes, may be harder than the cure of disease; because, while mortals love to sin, they do not love to be sick. Hence their comparative acquiescence in your endeavors to heal them of bodily ills, and their obstinate resistance to all efforts to save them from sin through Christ, spiritual Truth and Love, which redeem them, and become their Saviour, through the flesh, from the flesh,—the material world and evil.

This Life, Truth, and Love—this trinity of good—was individualized, to the perception of mortal sense, in the man Jesus. His history is emphatic in our hearts, and it lives more because of his spiritual than his physical healing. His example is, to Christian Scientists, what the models of the masters in music and painting are to artists.

Genuine Christian Scientists will no more deviate morally from that divine digest of Science called the Sermon on the Mount, than they will manipulate invalids, prescribe drugs, or deny God. Jesus' healing was spiritual in its nature, method, and design. He wrought the cure of disease through the divine Mind, which gives all true volition, impulse, and action; and destroys the mental error made manifest physically, and establishes the opposite manifestation of Truth upon the body in harmony and health.

By the individuality of God, do you mean that God has a finite form?

No. I mean the infinite and divine Principle of all being, the ever-present I AM, filling all space, including in itself all Mind, the one Father-Mother God. Life, Truth, and Love are this trinity in unity, and their universe is spiritual, peopled with perfect beings, harmonious and eternal, of which our material universe and men are the counterfeits.

Is God the Principle of all science, or only of Divine or Christian Science?

Science is Mind manifested. It is not material; neither is it of human origin.

All true Science represents a moral and spiritual force, which holds the earth in its orbit. This force is Spirit, that can "bind the sweet influences of the Pleiades," and "loose the bands of Orion."

There is no material science, if by that term you mean material intelligence. God is infinite Mind, hence there is no other Mind. Good is Mind, but evil is not Mind. Good is not in evil, but in God only. Spirit is not in matter, but in Spirit only. Law is not in matter, but in Mind only.

Is there no matter?

All is Mind. According to the Scriptures and Christian Science, all is God, and there is naught beside Him. "God is Spirit;" and we can only learn and love Him through His spirit, which brings out the fruits of Spirit and extinguishes forever the works of darkness by His marvellous light.

The five material senses testify to the existence of matter. The spiritual senses afford no such evidence, but deny the testimony of the material senses. Which testimony is correct? The Bible says: "Let God be true, and every man a liar." If, as the Scriptures imply, God is All-in-all, then all must be Mind, since God is Mind. Therefore in divine Science there is no material mortal man, for man is spiritual and eternal, he being made in the image of Spirit, or God.

There is no material sense. Matter is inert, inanimate, and sensationless,— considered apart from Mind. Lives there a man who has ever found Soul in the body or in matter, who has ever seen spiritual substance with the eye, who has found sight in matter, hearing in the material ear, or intelligence in non-intelligence? If there is any such thing as matter, it must be either mind which is called matter, or matter without Mind.

Matter without Mind is a moral impossibility. Mind in matter is pantheism. Soul is the only real consciousness which cognizes being. The body does not see, hear, smell, or taste. Human belief says that it does; but destroy this belief of seeing with the eye, and we could not see materially; and so it is with each of the physical senses.

Accepting the verdict of these material senses, we should believe man and the universe to be the football of chance and sinking into oblivion. Destroy the five senses as organized matter, and you must either become non-existent, or exist in Mind only; and this latter conclusion is the simple solution of the problem of being, and leads to the equal inference that there is no matter.

The sweet sounds and glories of earth and sky, assuming manifold forms and colors,—are they not tangible and material?

As Mind they are real, but not as matter. All beauty and goodness are in and of Mind, emanating from God; but when we change the nature of beauty and goodness from Mind to matter, the beauty is marred, through a false conception, and, to the material senses, evil takes the place of good.

Has not the truth in Christian Science met a response from Prof. S.P. Langley, the young American astronomer? He says that "color is in *us*," not "in the rose;" and he adds that this is not "any metaphysical subtlety," but a fact "almost universally accepted, within the *last few years*, by physicists."

Is not the basis of Mind-healing a destruction of the evidence of the material senses, and restoration of the true evidence of spiritual sense?

It is, so far as you perceive and understand this predicate and postulate of Mind-healing; but the Science of Mind-healing is best understood in practical demonstration. The proof of what you apprehend, in the simplest definite and absolute form of healing, can alone answer this question of how much you understand of Christian Science Mind-healing. Not that all healing is Science, by any means; but that the simplest case, healed in Science, is as demonstrably scientific, in a small degree, as the most difficult case so treated.

The infinite and subtler conceptions and consistencies of Christian Science are set forth in my work Science and Health.

Is man material or spiritual?

In Science, man is the manifest reflection of God, perfect and immortal Mind. He is the likeness of God; and His likeness would be lost if inverted or perverted.

According to the evidence of the so-called physical senses, man is material, fallen, sick, depraved, mortal. Science and spiritual sense contradict this, and they afford the only true evidence of the being of God and man, the material evidence being wholly false.

Jesus said of personal evil, that "the truth abode not in him," because there is no material sense. Matter, as matter, has neither sensation nor personal intelligence. As a pretension to be Mind, matter is a lie, and "the father of lies;" Mind is not in matter, and Spirit cannot originate its opposite, named matter.

According to divine Science, Spirit no more changes its species, by evolving matter from Spirit, than natural science, so-called, or material laws, bring about alteration of species by transforming minerals into vegetables or plants into animals,—thus confusing and confounding the three great kingdoms. No rock brings forth an apple; no pine-tree produces a mammal or provides breast-milk for babes.

To sense, the lion of to-day is the lion of six thousand years ago; but in Science, Spirit sends forth its own harmless likeness.

How should I undertake to demonstrate Christian Science in healing the sick?

As I have given you only an epitome of the Principle, so I can give you here nothing but an outline of the practice. Be honest, be true to thyself, and true to others; then it follows thou wilt be strong in God, the eternal good. Heal through Truth and Love; there is no other healer.

In all moral revolutions, from a lower to a higher condition of thought and action, Truth is in the minority and error has the majority. It is not otherwise in the field of Mind-healing. The man who calls himself a Christian Scientist, yet is false to God and man, is also uttering falsehood about good. This falsity shuts against him the Truth and the Principle of Science, but opens a way whereby, through will-power, sense may say the unchristian practitioner can heal; but Science shows that he makes morally worse the invalid whom he is supposed to cure.

By this I mean that mortal mind should not be falsely impregnated. If by such lower means the health is seemingly restored, the restoration is not lasting, and the patient is liable to a relapse,—"The last state of that man is worse than the first."

The teacher of Mind-healing who is not a Christian, in the highest sense, is constantly sowing the seeds of discord and disease. Even the truth he speaks is more or less blended with error; and this error will spring up in the mind of his pupil. The pupil's imperfect knowledge will lead to weakness in practice, and he will be a poor practitioner, if not a malpractitioner.

The basis of malpractice is in erring human will, and this will is an outcome of what I call *mortal mind,*—a false and temporal sense of Truth, Life, and Love. To heal, in Christian Science, is to base your practice on immortal Mind, the divine Principle of man's being; and this requires a preparation of the heart and an answer of the lips from the Lord.

The Science of healing is the Truth of healing. If one is untruthful, his mental state weighs against his healing power; and similar effects come from pride, envy, lust, and all fleshly vices.

The spiritual power of a scientific, right thought, without a direct effort, an audible or even a mental argument, has oftentimes healed inveterate diseases.

The thoughts of the practitioner should be imbued with a clear conviction of the omnipotence and omnipresence of God; that He is All, and that there can be none beside Him; that God is good, and the producer only of good; and hence, that whatever militates against health, harmony, or holiness, is an unjust usurper of the throne of the controller of all mankind. Note this, that if you have power in error, you forfeit the power that Truth bestows, and its salutary influence on yourself and others.

You must feel and know that God alone governs man; that His government is harmonious; that He is too pure to behold iniquity, and divides His power with nothing evil or material; that material laws are only human beliefs, which govern mortals wrongfully. These beliefs arise from the subjective states of thought, producing the beliefs of a mortal material universe,—so-called, and of material disease and mortality. Mortal ills are but errors of thought,—diseases of mortal mind, and not of matter; for matter cannot feel, see, or report pain or disease.

Disease is a thing of thought manifested on the body; and fear is the procurator of the thought which causes sickness and suffering. Remove this fear by the true sense that God is Love,—and that Love punishes nothing but sin,—and the patient can then look up to the loving God, and know that He afflicteth not willingly the children of men, who are punished because of disobedience to His spiritual law. His law of Truth, when obeyed, removes every erroneous physical and mental state. The belief that matter can master Mind, and make you ill, is an error which Truth will destroy.

You must learn to acknowledge God in all His ways. It is only a lack of understanding of the allness of God, which leads you to believe in the existence of matter, or that matter can frame its own conditions, contrary to the law of Spirit.

Sickness is the schoolmaster, leading you to Christ; first to faith in Christ; next to belief in God as omnipotent; and finally to the *understanding* of God and man in Christian Science, whereby you learn that God is good, and in Science man is His likeness, the forever reflection of goodness. Therefore good is one and All.

This brings forward the next proposition in Christian Science,—namely, that there are no sickness, sin, and death in the divine Mind. What seem to be disease, vice, and mortality are illusions of the physical senses. These illusions are not real, but unreal. Health is the consciousness of the unreality of pain and disease; or, rather, the absolute consciousness of harmony and of nothing else. In a moment you may awake from a night-dream; just so you can awake from the dream of sickness; but the demonstration of the Science of Mind-healing by no means rests on the strength of human belief. This demonstration is based on a true understanding of God and divine Science, which takes away every human belief, and, through the illumination of spiritual understanding, reveals the all-power and ever-presence of good, whence emanate health, harmony, and Life eternal.

The lecturer, teacher, or healer who is indeed a Christian Scientist, never introduces the subject of human anatomy; never depicts the muscular, vascular, or nervous operations of the human frame. He never talks about the structure of the material body. He never lays his hands on the patient, nor manipulates the parts of the body supposed to be ailing. Above all, he keeps unbroken the Ten Commandments, and practises Christ's Sermon on the Mount.

Wrong thoughts and methods strengthen the sense of disease, instead of cure it; or else quiet the fear of the sick on false grounds, encouraging them in the belief of error until they hold stronger than before the belief that they are first made sick by matter, and then restored through its agency. This fosters infidelity, and is mental quackery, that denies the Principle of Mind-healing. If the sick are aided in this mistaken fashion, their ailments will return, and be more stubborn because the relief is unchristian and unscientific.

Christian Science erases from the minds of invalids their mistaken belief that they live in or because of matter, or that a so-called material organism controls the health or existence of mankind, and induces rest in God, divine Love, as caring for all the conditions requisite for the well-being of man. As power divine is the healer, why should mortals concern themselves with the chemistry of food? Jesus said: "Take no thought what ye shall eat."

The practitioner should also endeavor to free the minds of the healthy from any sense of subordination to their bodies, and teach them that the divine Mind, not material law, maintains human health and life.

A Christian Scientist knows that, in Science, disease is unreal; that Mind is not in matter; that Life is God, good; hence Life is not functional, and is neither matter nor mortal mind; knows that pantheism and theosophy are not Science. Whatever saps, with human belief, this basis of Christian Science, renders it impossible to demonstrate the Principle of this Science, even in the smallest degree.

A mortal and material body is not the actual individuality of man made in the divine and spiritual image of God. The material body is not the likeness of Spirit; hence it is not the truth of being, but the likeness of error—the human belief which saith there is more than one God,—there is more than one Life and one Mind.

In Deuteronomy (iv. 35) we read: "The Lord, He is God; there is none else beside Him." In John (iv. 24) we may read: "God is Spirit." These propositions, understood in their Science, elucidate my meaning.

When treating a patient, it is not Science to treat every organ in the body. To aver that harmony is the real and discord is the unreal, and then give special attention to what according to their own belief is diseased, is scientific; and if the *healer realizes* the truth, it will free his patient.

What are the means and methods of trustworthy Christian Scientists?

These people should not be expected, more than others, to give all their time to Christian Science work, receiving no wages in return, but left to be fed, clothed, and sheltered by charity. Neither can they serve two masters, giving only a portion of their time to God, and still be Christian Scientists. They must give Him all their services, and "owe no man." To do this, they must at present ask a suitable price for their services, and then *conscientiously earn their wages*, strictly practising Divine Science, and healing the sick.

The author never sought charitable support, but gave fully seven-eighths of her time without remuneration, except the bliss of doing good. The only pay taken for her labors was from classes, and often those were put off for months, in order to do gratuitous work. She has never taught a Primary class without several, and sometimes seventeen, free students in it; and has endeavored to take the full price of tuition only from those who were able to pay. The student who pays must of necessity do better than he who does not pay, and yet will expect and require others to pay him. No discount on tuition was made on higher classes, because their first classes furnished students with the means of paying for their tuition in the higher instruction, and of doing charity work besides. If the Primary students are still impecunious, it is their own fault, and this ill-success of itself leaves them unprepared to enter higher classes.

People are being healed by means of my instructions, both in and out of class. Many students, who have passed through a regular course of instruction from me, have been invalids and were healed in the class; but experience has shown that this defrauds the scholar, though it heals the sick.

It is seldom that a student, if healed in a class, has left it understanding sufficiently the Science of healing to immediately enter upon its practice. Why? Because the glad surprise of suddenly regained health is a shock to the mind; and this holds and satisfies the thought with exuberant joy.

This renders the mind less inquisitive, plastic, and tractable; and deep systematic thinking is impracticable until this impulse subsides.

This was the principal reason for advising diseased people not to enter a class. Few were taken besides invalids for students, until there were enough practitioners to fill in the best possible manner the department of healing. Teaching and healing should have separate departments, and these should be fortified on all sides with suitable and thorough guardianship and grace.

Only a very limited number of students can advantageously enter a class, grapple with this subject, and well assimilate what has been taught them. It is impossible to teach thorough Christian Science to promiscuous and large assemblies, or to persons who cannot be addressed individually, so that the mind of the pupil may be dissected more critically than the body of a subject laid bare for anatomical examination. Public lectures cannot be such lessons in Christian Science as are required to empty and to fill anew the individual mind.

If publicity and material control are the motives for teaching, then public lectures can take the place of private lessons; but the former can never give a thorough knowledge of Christian Science, and a Christian Scientist will never undertake to fit students for practice by such means. Lectures in public are needed, but they must be subordinate to thorough class instruction in any branch of education.

None with an imperfect sense of the spiritual signification of the Bible, and its scientific relation to Mind-healing, should attempt overmuch in their translation of the Scriptures into the "new tongue;" but I see that some novices, in the truth of Science, and some impostors are committing this error.

Is there more than one school of scientific healing?

In reality there is, and can be, but one school of the Science of Mind-healing. Any departure from Science is an irreparable loss of Science. Whatever is said and written correctly on this Science originates from the Principle and practice laid down in Science and Health, a work which I published in 1875. This was the first book, recorded in history, which elucidates a pathological Science purely mental.

Minor shades of difference in Mind-healing have originated with certain opposing factions, springing up among unchristian students, who, fusing with a class of aspirants which snatch at whatever is progressive, call it their first-fruits, or else *post mortem* evidence.

A slight divergence is fatal in Science. Like certain Jews whom St. Paul had hoped to convert from mere motives of self-aggrandizement to the love of Christ, these so-called schools are clogging the wheels of progress by blinding the people to the true character of Christian Science,—its moral power, and its divine efficacy to heal.

The true understanding of Christian Science Mind-healing never originated in pride, rivalry, or the deification of self. The Discoverer of this Science could tell you of timidity, of self-distrust, of friendlessness, toil, agonies, and victories under which she needed miraculous vision to sustain her, when taking the first footsteps in this Science.

The ways of Christianity have not changed. Meekness, selflessness, and love are the paths of His testimony and the footsteps of His flock.

UNITY OF GOOD

BY

MARY BAKER EDDY

Contents

Unity of Good

Caution in the Truth

Perhaps no doctrine of Christian Science rouses so much natural doubt and questioning as this, that God knows no such thing as sin. Indeed, this may be set down as one of the "things hard to be understood," such as the apostle Peter declared were taught by his fellow-apostle Paul, "which they that are unlearned and unstable wrest ... unto their own destruction." (2 Peter iii. 16.)

Let us then reason together on this important subject, whose statement in Christian Science may justly be characterized as *wonderful*.

Does God know or behold sin, sickness, and death?

The nature and character of God is so little apprehended and demonstrated by mortals, that I counsel my students to defer this infinite inquiry, in their discussions of Christian Science. In fact, they had better leave the subject untouched, until they draw nearer to the divine character, and are practically able to testify, by their lives, that as they come closer to the true understanding of God they lose all sense of error.

The Scriptures declare that God is too pure to behold iniquity (Habakkuk i. 13); but they also declare that God pitieth them who fear Him; that there is no place where His voice is not heard; that He is "a very present help in trouble."

The sinner has no refuge from sin, except in God, who is his salvation. We must, however, realize God's presence, power, and love, in order to be saved from sin. This realization takes away man's fondness for sin and his pleasure in it; and, lastly, it removes the pain which accrues to him from it. Then follows this, as the *finale* in Science: The sinner loses his sense of sin, and gains a higher sense of God, in whom there is no sin.

The true man, really *saved*, is ready to testify of God in the infinite penetration of Truth, and can affirm that the Mind which is good, or God, has no knowledge of sin.

In the same manner the sick lose their sense of sickness, and gain that spiritual sense of harmony which contains neither discord nor disease.

According to this same rule, in divine Science, the dying—if they die in the Lord—awake from a sense of death to a sense of Life in Christ, with a knowledge of Truth and Love beyond what they possessed before; because their lives have grown so far toward the stature of manhood in Christ Jesus, that they are ready for a spiritual transfiguration, through their affections and understanding.

Those who reach this transition, called *death*, without having rightly improved the lessons of this primary school of mortal existence,—and still believe in matter's reality, pleasure, and pain,—are not ready to understand immortality. Hence they awake only to another sphere of experience, and must pass through another probationary state before it can be truly said of them: "Blessed are the dead which die in the Lord."

They upon whom the second death, of which we read in the Apocalypse (Revelation xx. 6), hath no power, are those who have obeyed God's commands, and have washed their robes white through the sufferings of the flesh and the triumphs of Spirit. Thus they have reached the goal in divine Science, by knowing Him in whom they have believed. This knowledge is not the forbidden fruit of sin, sickness, and death, but it is the fruit which grows on the "tree of life." This is the understanding of God, whereby man is found in the image and likeness of good, not of evil; of health, not of sickness; of Life, not of death.

God is All-in-all. Hence He is in Himself only, in His own nature and character, and is perfect being, or consciousness. He is all the Life and Mind there is or can be. Within Himself is every embodiment of Life and Mind.

If He is All, He can have no consciousness of anything unlike Himself; because, if He is omnipresent, there can be nothing outside of Himself.

Now this self-same God is our helper. He pities us. He has mercy upon us, and guides every event of our careers. He is near to them who adore Him. To understand Him, without a single taint of our mortal, finite sense of sin, sickness, or death, is to approach Him and become like Him.

Truth is God, and in God's law. This law declares that Truth is All, and there is no error. This law of Truth destroys every phase of error. To gain a temporary consciousness of God's law is to feel, in a certain finite human sense, that God comes to us and pities us; but the attainment of the understanding of His presence, through the Science of God, destroys our sense of imperfection, or of His absence, through a diviner sense that God is all true consciousness; and this convinces us that, as we get still nearer Him, we must forever lose our own consciousness of error.

But how could we lose all consciousness of error, if God be conscious of it? God has not forbidden man to know Him; on the contrary, the Father bids man have the same Mind "which was also in Christ Jesus,"—which was certainly the divine Mind; but God does forbid man's acquaintance with evil. Why? Because evil is no part of the divine knowledge.

John's Gospel declares (xvii. 3) that "life eternal" consists in the knowledge of the only true God, and of Jesus Christ, whom He has sent. Surely from such an understanding of Science, such knowing, the vision of sin is wholly excluded.

Nevertheless, at the present crude hour, no wise men or women will rudely or prematurely agitate a theme involving the All of infinity.

Rather will they rejoice in the small understanding they have already gained of the wholeness of Deity, and work gradually and gently up toward the perfect thought divine. This meekness will increase their apprehension of God, because their mental struggles and pride of opinion will proportionately diminish.

Every one should be encouraged not to accept any personal opinion on so great a matter, but to seek the divine Science of this question of Truth by following upward individual convictions, undisturbed by the frightened sense of any need of attempting to solve every Life-problem in a day.

"Great is the mystery of godliness," says Paul; and *mystery* involves the unknown. No stubborn purpose to force conclusions on this subject will unfold in us a higher sense of Deity; neither will it promote the Cause of Truth or enlighten the individual thought.

Let us respect the rights of conscience and the liberty of the sons of God, so letting our "moderation be known to all men." Let no enmity, no untempered controversy, spring up between Christian Science students and Christians who wholly or partially differ from them as to the nature of sin and the marvellous unity of man with God shadowed forth in scientific thought. Rather let the stately goings of this wonderful part of Truth be left to the supernal guidance.

"These are but parts of Thy ways," says Job; and the whole is greater than its parts. Our present understanding is but "the seed within itself," for it is divine Science, "bearing fruit after its kind."

Sooner or later the whole human race will learn that, in proportion as the spotless selfhood of God is understood, human nature will be renovated, and man will receive a higher selfhood, derived from God, and the redemption of mortals from sin, sickness, and death be established on everlasting foundations.

The Science of physical harmony, as now presented to the people in divine light, is radical enough to promote as forcible collisions of thought as the age has strength to bear. Until the heavenly law of health, according to Christian Science, is firmly grounded, even the thinkers are not prepared to answer intelligently leading questions about God and sin, and the world is far from ready to assimilate such a grand and all-absorbing verity concerning the divine nature and character as is embraced in the theory of God's blindness to error and ignorance of sin. No wise mother, though a graduate of Wellesley College, will talk to her babe about the problems of Euclid.

Not much more than a half-century ago the assertion of universal salvation provoked discussion and horror, similar to what our declarations about sin and Deity must arouse, if hastily pushed to the front while the platoons of Christian Science are not yet thoroughly drilled in the plainer manual of their spiritual armament. "Wait patiently on the Lord;" and in less than another fifty years His name will be magnified in the apprehension of this new subject, as already He is glorified in the wide extension of belief in the impartial grace of God,—shown by the changes at Andover Seminary and in multitudes of other religious folds.

Nevertheless, though I thus speak, and from my heart of hearts, it is due both to Christian Science and myself to make also the following statement: When I have most clearly seen and most sensibly felt that the infinite recognizes no disease, this has not separated me from God, but has so bound me to Him as to enable me instantaneously to heal a cancer which had eaten its way to the jugular vein.

In the same spiritual condition I have been able to replace dislocated joints and raise the dying to instantaneous health. People are now living who can bear witness to these cures. Herein is my evidence, from on high, that the views here promulgated on this subject are correct.

Certain self-proved propositions pour into my waiting thought in connection with these experiences; and here is one such conviction: that an acknowledgment of the perfection of the infinite Unseen confers a power nothing else can. An incontestable point in divine Science is, that because God is All, a realization of this fact dispels even the sense or consciousness of sin, and brings us nearer to God, bringing out the highest phenomena of the All-Mind.

Seedtime and Harvest

Let another query now be considered, which gives much trouble to many earnest thinkers before Science answers it.

Is anything real of which the physical senses are cognizant?

Everything is as real as you make it, and no more so. What you see, hear, feel, is a mode of consciousness, and can have no other reality than the sense you entertain of it.

It is dangerous to rest upon the evidence of the senses, for this evidence is not absolute, and therefore not real, in our sense of the word. All that is beautiful and good in your individual consciousness is permanent. That which is not so is illusive and fading. My insistence upon a proper understanding of the unreality of matter and evil arises from their deleterious effects, physical, moral, and intellectual, upon the race.

All forms of error are uprooted in Science, on the same basis whereby sickness is healed,—namely, by the establishment, through reason, revelation, and Science, of the nothingness of every claim of error, even the doctrine of heredity and other physical causes. You demonstrate the process of Science, and it proves my view conclusively, that mortal mind is the cause of all disease. Destroy the mental sense of the disease, and the disease itself disappears. Destroy the sense of sin, and sin itself disappears.

Material and sensual consciousness are mortal. Hence they must, some time and in some way, be reckoned unreal. That time has partially come, or my words would not have been spoken. Jesus has made the way plain,—so plain that all are without excuse who walk not in it; but this way is not the path of physical science, human philosophy, or mystic psychology.

The talent and genius of the centuries have wrongly reckoned. They have not based upon revelation their arguments and conclusions as to the source and resources of being,—its combinations, phenomena, and outcome,—but have built instead upon the sand of human reason. They have not accepted the simple teaching and life of Jesus as the only true solution of the perplexing problem of human existence.

Sometimes it is said, by those who fail to understand me, that I *monopolize*; and this is said because ideas akin to mine have been held by a few spiritual thinkers in all ages. So they have, but in a far different form. Healing has gone on continually; yet healing, as I teach it, has not been practised since the days of Christ.

What is the cardinal point of the difference in my metaphysical system? This: that *by knowing the unreality of disease, sin, and death*, you demonstrate the allness of God. This difference wholly separates my system from all others. The reality of these so-called existences I deny, because they are not to be found in God, and this system is built on Him as the sole cause. It would be difficult to name any previous teachers, save Jesus and his apostles, who have thus taught.

If there be any *monopoly* in my teaching, it lies in this utter reliance upon the one God, to whom belong all things.

Life is God, or Spirit, the supersensible eternal. The universe and man are the spiritual phenomena of this one infinite Mind. Spiritual phenomena never converge toward aught but infinite Deity. Their gradations are spiritual and divine; they cannot collapse, or lapse into their opposites, for God is their divine Principle. They live, because He lives; and they are eternally perfect, because He is perfect, and governs them in the Truth of divine Science, whereof God is the Alpha and Omega, the centre and circumference.

To attempt the calculation of His mighty ways, from the evidence before the material senses, is fatuous. It is like commencing with the minus sign, to learn the principle of positive mathematics.

God was not in the whirlwind. He is not the blind force of a material universe. Mortals must learn this; unless, pursued by their fears, they would endeavor to hide from His presence under their own falsities, and call in vain for the mountains of unholiness to shield them from the penalty of error.

Jesus taught us to walk *over*, not *into* or *with*, the currents of matter, or mortal mind. His teachings beard the lions in their dens. He turned the water into wine, he commanded the winds, he healed the sick,—all in direct opposition to human philosophy and so-called natural science. He annulled the laws of matter, showing them to be laws of mortal mind, not of God. He showed the need of changing this mind and its abortive laws. He demanded a change of consciousness and evidence, and effected this change through the higher laws of God. The palsied hand moved, despite the boastful sense of physical law and order. Jesus stooped not to human consciousness, nor to the evidence of the senses. He heeded not the taunt, "That withered hand looks very real and feels very real;" but he cut off this vain boasting and destroyed human pride by taking away the material evidence. If his patient was a theologian of some bigoted sect, a physician, or a professor of natural philosophy,—according to the ruder sort then prevalent,—he never thanked Jesus for restoring his senseless hand; but neither red tape nor indignity hindered the divine process. Jesus required neither cycles of time nor thought in order to mature fitness for perfection and its possibilities. He said that the kingdom of heaven is here, and is included in Mind; that while ye say, There are yet four months, and *then* cometh the harvest, I say, Look up, not down, for your fields are already white for the harvest; and gather the harvest by mental, not material processes. The laborers are few in this vineyard of Mind-sowing and reaping; but let them apply to the waiting grain the curving sickle of Mind's eternal circle, and bind it with bands of Soul.

The Deep Things of God

Science reverses the evidence of the senses in theology, on the same principle that it does in astronomy. Popular theology makes God tributary to man, coming at human call; whereas the reverse is true in Science. Men must approach God reverently, doing their own work in obedience to divine law, if they would fulfil the intended harmony of being.

The principle of music knows nothing of discord. God is harmony's selfhood. His universal laws, His unchangeableness, are not infringed in ethics any more than in music. To Him there is no moral inharmony; as we shall learn, proportionately as we gain the true understanding of Deity. If God could be conscious of sin, His infinite power would straightway reduce the universe to chaos.

If God has any real knowledge of sin, sickness, and death, they must be eternal; since He is, in the very fibre of His being, "without beginning of years or end of days." If God knows that which is not permanent, it follows that He knows something which He must learn to *unknow*, for the benefit of our race.

Such a view would bring us upon an outworn theological platform, which contains such planks as the divine repentance, and the belief that God must one day do His work over again, because it was not at first done aright.

Can it be seriously held, by any thinker, that long after God made the universe,—earth, man, animals, plants, the sun, the moon, and "the stars also,"—He should so gain wisdom and power from past experience that He could vastly improve upon His own previous work,—as Burgess, the boatbuilder, remedies in the Volunteer the shortcomings of the Puritan's model?

Christians are commanded to *grow in grace*. Was it necessary for God to grow in grace, that He might rectify His spiritual universe?

The Jehovah of limited Hebrew faith might need repentance, because His created children proved sinful; but the New Testament tells us of "the Father of lights, with whom is no variableness, neither shadow of turning." God is not the shifting vane on the spire, but the corner-stone of living rock, firmer than everlasting hills.

As God is Mind, if this Mind is familiar with evil, all cannot be good therein. Our infinite model would be taken away. What is in eternal Mind must be reflected in man, Mind's image. How then could man escape, or hope to escape, from a knowledge which is everlasting in his creator?

God never said that man would become better by learning to distinguish evil from good,—but the contrary, that by this knowledge, by man's first disobedience, came "death into the world, and all our woe."

"Shall mortal man be more just than God?" asks the poet-patriarch. May men rid themselves of an incubus which God never can throw off? Do mortals know more than God, that they may declare Him absolutely cognizant of sin?

God created all things, and pronounced them good. Was evil among these good things? Man is God's child and image. If God knows evil, so must man, or the likeness is incomplete, the image marred.

If man must be destroyed by the knowledge of evil, then his destruction comes through the very knowledge caught from God, and the creature is punished for his likeness to his creator.

God is commonly called the *sinless*, and man the *sinful*; but if the thought of sin could be possible in Deity, would Deity then be sinless? Would God not of necessity take precedence as the infinite sinner, and human sin become only an echo of the divine?

Such vagaries are to be found in heathen religious history. There are, or have been, devotees who worship not the good Deity, who will not harm them, but the bad deity, who seeks to do them mischief, and whom therefore they wish to bribe with prayers into quiescence, as a criminal appeases, with a money-bag, the venal officer.

Surely this is no Christian worship! In Christianity man bows to the infinite perfection which he is bidden to imitate. In Truth, such terms as *divine sin* and *infinite sinner* are unheard-of contradictions,—absurdities; but *would* they be sheer nonsense, if God has, or can have, a real knowledge of sin?

Ways Higher than Our Ways

A lie has only one chance of successful deception,—to be accounted true. Evil seeks to fasten all error upon God, and so make the lie seem part of eternal Truth.

Emerson says, "Hitch your wagon to a star." I say, Be allied to the deific power, and all that is good will aid your journey, as the stars in their courses fought against Sisera. (Judges v. 20.) Hourly, in Christian Science, man thus weds himself with God, or rather he ratifies a union predestined from all eternity; but evil ties its wagon-load of offal to the divine chariots,—or seeks so to do,—that its vileness may be christened purity, and its darkness get consolation from borrowed scintillations.

Jesus distinctly taught the arrogant Pharisees that, from the beginning, their father, the devil, was the would-be murderer of Truth. A right apprehension of the wonderful utterances of him who "spake as never man spake," would despoil error of its borrowed plumes, and transform the universe into a home of marvellous light,—"a consummation devoutly to be wished."

Error says God must know evil because He knows all things; but Holy Writ declares God told our first parents that in the day when they should partake of the fruit of evil, they must surely die. Would it not absurdly follow that God must perish, if He knows evil and evil necessarily leads to extinction? Rather let us think of God as saying, I am infinite good; therefore I know not evil. Dwelling in light, I can see only the brightness of My own glory.

Error may say that God can never save man from sin, if He knows and sees it not; but God says, I am too pure to behold iniquity, and destroy everything that is unlike Myself.

Many fancy that our heavenly Father reasons thus: If pain and sorrow were not in My mind, I could not remedy them, and wipe the tears from the eyes of My children. Error says you must know grief in order to console it. Truth, God, says you oftenest console others in troubles that you have not. Is not our comforter always from outside and above ourselves?

God says, I show My pity through divine law, not through human. It is My sympathy with and My knowledge of harmony (not inharmony) which alone enable Me to rebuke, and eventually destroy, every supposition of discord.

Error says God must know death in order to strike at its root; but God saith, I am ever-conscious Life, and thus I conquer death; for to be ever conscious of

Life is to be never conscious of death. I am All. A knowledge of aught beside Myself is impossible.

If such knowledge of evil were possible to God, it would lower His rank.

With God, *knowledge* is necessarily *foreknowledge*; and *foreknowledge* and *foreordination* must be one, in an infinite Being. What Deity *foreknows*, Deity must *foreordain*; else He is not omnipotent, and, like ourselves, He foresees events which are contrary to His creative will, yet which He cannot avert.

If God knows evil at all, He must have had foreknowledge thereof; and if He foreknew it, He must virtually have intended it, or ordered it aforetime,—foreordained it; else how could it have come into the world?

But this we cannot believe of God; for if the supreme good could predestine or foreknow evil, there would be sin in Deity, and this would be the end of infinite moral unity. "If therefore the light that is in thee be darkness, how great is that darkness!" On the contrary, evil is only a delusive deception, without any actuality which Truth can know.

Rectifications

How is a mistake to be rectified? By reversal or revision,—by seeing it in its proper light, and then turning it or turning from it.

We undo the statements of error by reversing them.

Through these three statements, or misstatements, evil comes into authority:—

First: The Lord created it.
Second: The Lord knows it.
Third: I am afraid of it.

By a reverse process of argument evil must be dethroned:—

First: God never made evil.
Second: He knows it not.
Third: We therefore need not fear it.

Try this process, dear inquirer, and so reach that perfect Love which "casteth out fear," and then see if this Love does not destroy in you all hate and the sense of evil. You will awake to the perception of God as All-in-all. You will find yourself losing the knowledge and the operation of sin, proportionably as you realize the divine infinitude and believe that He can see nothing outside of His own focal distance.

A Colloquy

In Romans (ii. 15) we read the apostle's description of mental processes wherein human thoughts are "the mean while accusing or else excusing one another." If we observe our mental processes, we shall find that we are perpetually arguing with ourselves; yet each mortal is not two personalities, but one.

In like manner good and evil talk to one another; yet they are not two but one, for evil is naught, and good only is reality.

Evil. God hath said, "Ye shall eat of every tree of the garden." If you do not, your intellect will be circumscribed and the evidence of your personal senses be denied. This would antagonize individual consciousness and existence.

Good. The Lord is God. With Him is no consciousness of evil, because there is nothing beside Him or outside of Him. Individual consciousness in man is inseparable from good. There is no sensible matter, no sense in matter; but there is a spiritual sense, a sense of Spirit, and this is the only consciousness belonging to true individuality, or a divine sense of being.

Evil. Why is this so?

Good. Because man is made after God's eternal likeness, and this likeness consists in a sense of harmony and immortality, in which no evil can possibly dwell. You may eat of the fruit of Godlikeness, but as to the fruit of ungodliness, which is opposed to Truth,—ye shall not touch it, lest ye die.

Evil. But I would taste and know error for myself.

Good. Thou shalt not admit that error is something to know or be known, to eat or be eaten, to see or be seen, to feel or be felt. To admit the existence of error would be to admit the truth of a lie.

Evil. But there is something besides good. God knows that a knowledge of this something is essential to happiness and life. A lie is as genuine as Truth, though not so legitimate a child of God. Whatever exists must come from God, and be important to our knowledge. Error, even, is His offspring.

Good. Whatever cometh not from the eternal Spirit, has its origin in the physical senses and material brains, called *human intellect* and *will-power,—alias* intelligent matter.

In Shakespeare's tragedy of King Lear, it was the traitorous and cruel treatment received by old Gloster from his bastard son Edmund which makes true the lines:
The gods are just, and of our pleasant vices
Make instruments to scourge us.

His lawful son, Edgar, was to his father ever loyal. Now God has no bastards to turn again and rend their Maker. The divine children are born of law and order, and Truth knows only such.

How well the Shakespearean tale agrees with the word of Scripture, in Hebrews xii. 7, 8: "If ye endure chastening, God dealeth with you as with sons; for what son is he whom the father chasteneth not? But if ye be without chastisement, whereof all are partakers, then are ye bastards, and not sons."

The doubtful or spurious evidence of the senses is not to be admitted,— especially when they testify concerning Spirit, whereof they are confessedly incompetent to speak.

Evil. But mortal mind and sin really exist!

Good. How can they exist, unless God has created them? And how can He create anything so wholly unlike Himself and foreign to His nature? An evil material mind, so-called, can conceive of God only as like itself, and knowing both evil and good; but a purely good and spiritual consciousness has no sense whereby to cognize evil. Mortal mind is the opposite of immortal Mind, and sin the opposite of goodness. I am the infinite All. From me proceedeth all Mind, all consciousness, all individuality, all being. My Mind is divine good, and cannot drift into evil. To believe in minds many is to depart from the supreme sense of harmony. Your assumptions insist that there is more than the one Mind, more than the one God; but verily I say unto you, God is All-in-all; and you can never be outside of His oneness.

Evil. I am a finite consciousness, a material individuality,—a mind in matter, which is both evil and good.

Good. All consciousness is Mind; and Mind is God,—an infinite, and not a finite consciousness. This consciousness is reflected in individual consciousness, or man, whose source is infinite Mind. There is no really finite mind, no finite consciousness. There is no material substance, for Spirit is all that endureth, and hence is the only substance. There is, can be, no evil mind, because Mind is God. God and His ideas—that is, God and the universe—constitute all that exists. Man, as God's offspring, must be spiritual, perfect, eternal.

Evil. I am something separate from good or God. I am substance. My mind is more than matter. In my mortal mind, matter becomes conscious, and is able to see, taste, hear, feel, smell. Whatever matter thus affirms is mainly correct. If you, O good, deny this, then I deny your truthfulness. If you say that matter is unconscious, you stultify my intellect, insult my conscience, and dispute self-evident facts; for nothing can be clearer than the testimony of the five senses.

Good. Spirit is the only substance. Spirit is God, and God is good; hence good is the only substance, the only Mind. Mind is not, cannot be, in matter. It sees, hears, feels, tastes, smells as Mind, and not as matter. Matter cannot talk; and hence, whatever it appears to say of itself is a lie. This lie, that Mind can be in matter,—claiming to be something beside God, denying Truth and its demonstration in Christian Science,—this lie I declare an illusion. This denial enlarges the human intellect by removing its evidence from sense to Soul, and from finiteness into infinity. It honors conscious human individuality by showing God as its source.

Evil. I am a creator,—but upon a material, not a spiritual basis. I give life, and I can destroy life.

Good. Evil is not a creator. God, good, is the only creator. Evil is not conscious or conscientious Mind; it is not individual, not actual. Evil is not spiritual, and therefore has no groundwork in Life, whose only source is Spirit. The elements which belong to the eternal All,—Life, Truth, Love,—evil can never take away.

Evil. I am intelligent matter; and matter is egoistic, having its own innate selfhood and the capacity to evolve mind. God is in matter, and matter reproduces God. From Him come my forms, near or remote. This is my honor, that God is my author, authority, governor, disposer. I am proud to be in His outstretched hands, and I shirk all responsibility for myself as evil, and for my varying manifestations.

Good. You mistake, O evil! God is not your authority and law. Neither is He the author of the material changes, the *phantasma*, a belief in which leads to such teaching as we find in the hymn-verse so often sung in church:—

> Chance and change are busy ever,
> Man decays and ages move;
> But His mercy waneth never,—
> God is wisdom, God is love.

Now if it be true that God's power *never waneth*, how can it be also true that *chance* and *change* are universal factors,—that *man decays*? Many ordinary Christians protest against this stanza of Bowring's, and its sentiment is foreign to Christian Science. If God be *changeless goodness*, as sings another line of this hymn, what place has *chance* in the divine economy? Nay, there is in God naught fantastic. All is real, all is serious. The phantasmagoria is a product of human dreams.

The Ego

From various friends comes inquiry as to the meaning of a word employed in the foregoing colloquy.

There are two English words, often used as if they were synonyms, which really have a shade of difference between them.

An *egotist* is one who talks much of himself. *Egotism* implies vanity and self-conceit.

Egoism is a more philosophical word, signifying a passionate love of self, which doubts all existence except its own. An *egoist*, therefore, is one uncertain of everything except his own existence.

Applying these distinctions to evil and God, we shall find that evil is *egotistic*,—boastful, but fleeing like a shadow at daybreak; while God is *egoistic*, knowing only His own all-presence, all-knowledge, all-power.

Soul

We read in the Hebrew Scriptures, "The soul that sinneth, it shall die."

What is Soul? Is it a reality within the mortal body? Who can prove that? Anatomy has not descried nor described Soul. It was never touched by the scalpel nor cut with the dissecting-knife. The five physical senses do not cognize it.

Who, then, dares define Soul as something within man? As well might you declare some old castle to be peopled with demons or angels, though never a light or form was discerned therein, and not a spectre had ever been seen going in or coming out.

The common hypotheses about souls are even more vague than ordinary material conjectures, and have less basis; because material theories are built on the evidence of the material senses.

Soul must be God; since we learn Soul only as we learn God, by spiritualization. As the five senses take no cognizance of Soul, so they take no cognizance of God. Whatever cannot be taken in by mortal mind—by human reflection, reason, or belief—must be the unfathomable Mind, which "eye hath not seen, nor ear heard." Soul stands in this relation to every hypothesis as to its human character.

If Soul sins, it is a sinner, and Jewish law condemned the sinner to death,— as does all criminal law, to a certain extent.

Spirit never sins, because Spirit is God. Hence, as Spirit, Soul is sinless, and is God. Therefore there is, there can be, no spiritual death.

Transcending the evidence of the material senses, Science declares God to be the Soul of all being, the only Mind and intelligence in the universe. There is but one God, one Soul, or Mind, and that one is infinite, supplying all that is absolutely immutable and eternal,—Truth, Life, Love.

Science reveals Soul as that which the senses cannot define from any standpoint of their own. What the physical senses miscall soul, Christian Science defines as material sense; and herein lies the discrepancy between the true Science of Soul and that material sense of a soul which that very sense declares can never be seen or measured or weighed or touched by physicality.

Often we can elucidate the deep meaning of the Scriptures by reading *sense* instead of *soul*, as in the Forty-second Psalm: "Why art thou cast down, O my soul [sense]?... Hope thou in God [Soul]: for I shall yet praise Him, who is the health of my countenance, and my God [my Soul, immortality]."

The Virgin-mother's sense being uplifted to behold Spirit as the sole origin of man, she exclaimed, "My soul [spiritual sense] doth magnify the Lord."

Human language constantly uses the word *soul* for *sense*. This it does under the delusion that the senses can reverse the spiritual facts of Science, whereas Science reverses the testimony of the material senses.

Soul is Life, and being spiritual Life, never sins. Material sense is the so-called material life. Hence this lower sense sins and suffers, according to material belief, till divine understanding takes away this belief and restores Soul, or spiritual Life. "He restoreth my soul," says David.

In his first epistle to the Corinthians (xv. 45) Paul writes: "The first man Adam was made a living soul; the last Adam was made a quickening spirit." The apostle refers to the second Adam as the Messiah, our blessed Master, whose interpretation of God and His creation—by restoring the spiritual sense of man as immortal instead of mortal—made humanity victorious over death and the grave.

When I discovered the power of Spirit to break the cords of matter, through a change in the mortal sense of things, then I discerned the last Adam as a quickening Spirit, and understood the meaning of the declaration of Holy Writ, "The first shall be last,"—the living Soul shall be found a quickening Spirit; or, rather, shall reflect the Life of the divine Arbiter.

There is no Matter

"God is a Spirit" (or, more accurately translated, "God is Spirit"), declares the Scripture (John iv. 24), "and they that worship Him must worship Him in spirit and in truth."

If God is Spirit, and God is All, surely there can be no matter; for the divine All must be Spirit.

The tendency of Christianity is to spiritualize thought and action. The demonstrations of Jesus annulled the claims of matter, and overruled laws material as emphatically as they annihilated sin.

According to Christian Science, the *first* idolatrous claim of sin is, that matter exists; the *second*, that matter is substance; the *third*, that matter has intelligence; and the *fourth*, that matter, being so endowed, produces life and death.

Hence my conscientious position, in the denial of matter, rests on the fact that matter usurps the authority of God, Spirit; and the nature and character of matter, the antipode of Spirit, include all that denies and defies Spirit, in quantity or quality.

This subject can be enlarged. It can be shown, in detail, that evil does not obtain in Spirit, God; and that God, or good, is Spirit alone; whereas, evil *does*, according to belief, obtain in matter; and that evil is a false claim,—false to God, false to Truth and Life. Hence the claim of matter usurps the prerogative of God, saying, "I am a creator. God made me, and I make man and the material universe."

Spirit is the only creator, and man, including the universe, is His spiritual concept. By matter is commonly meant mind,—not the highest Mind, but a false form of mind. This so-called mind and matter cannot be separated in origin and action.

What is this mind? It is not the Mind of Spirit; for spiritualization of thought destroys all sense of matter as substance, Life, or intelligence, and enthrones God in the eternal qualities of His being.

This lower, misnamed mind is a false claim, a suppositional mind, which I prefer to call *mortal mind*. True Mind is immortal. This mortal mind declares itself material, in sin, sickness, and death, virtually saying, "I am the opposite of Spirit, of holiness, harmony, and Life."

To this declaration Christian Science responds, even as did our Master: "You were a murderer from the beginning. The truth abode not in you. You are a liar, and the father of it." Here it appears that a *liar* was in the neuter gender,— neither masculine nor feminine. Hence it was not man (the image of God) who lied, but the false claim to personality, which I call *mortal mind*; a claim which Christian Science uncovers, in order to demonstrate the falsity of the claim.

There are lesser arguments which prove matter to be identical with mortal mind, and this mind a lie.

The physical senses (matter really having no sense) give the only pretended testimony there can be as to the existence of a substance called *matter*. Now these senses, being material, can only testify from their own evidence, and concerning themselves; yet we have it on divine authority: "If I bear witness of myself, my witness is not true." (John v. 31.)

In other words: matter testifies of itself, "I am matter;" but unless matter is mind, it cannot talk or testify; and if it is mind, it is certainly not the Mind of Christ, not the Mind that is identical with Truth.

Brain, thus assuming to testify, is only matter within the skull, and is believed to be mind only through error and delusion. Examine that form of matter called *brains*, and you find no mind therein. Hence the logical sequence, that there is in reality neither matter nor mortal mind, but that the self-testimony of the physical senses is false.

Examine these witnesses for error, or falsity, and observe the foundations of their testimony, and you will find them divided in evidence, mocking the Scripture (Matthew xviii. 16), "In the mouth of two or three witnesses every word may be established."

Sight. Mortal mind declares that matter sees through the organizations of matter, or that mind sees by means of matter. Disorganize the so-called material structure, and then mortal mind says, "I cannot see;" and declares that matter is the master of mind, and that non-intelligence governs. Mortal mind admits that it sees only material images, pictured on the eye's retina.

What then is the line of the syllogism? It must be this: That matter is not seen; that mortal mind cannot see without matter; and therefore that the whole function of material sight is an illusion, a lie.

Here comes in the summary of the whole matter, wherewith we started: that God is All, and God is Spirit; therefore there is nothing but Spirit; and consequently there is no matter.

Touch. Take another train of reasoning. Mortal mind says that matter cannot feel matter; yet put your finger on a burning coal, and the nerves, material nerves, *do* feel matter.

Again I ask: What evidence does mortal mind afford that matter is substantial, is hot or cold? Take away mortal mind, and matter could not feel what it calls *substance.* Take away matter, and mortal mind could not cognize its own so-called substance, and this so-called mind would have no identity. Nothing would remain to be seen or felt.

What is substance? What is the reality of God and the universe? Immortal Mind is the real substance,—Spirit, Life, Truth, and Love.

Taste. Mortal mind says, "I taste; and this is sweet, this is sour." Let mortal mind change, and say that sour is sweet, and so it would be. If every mortal mind believed sweet to be sour, it would be so; for the qualities of matter are but qualities of mortal mind. Change the mind, and the quality changes. Destroy the belief, and the quality disappears.

The so-called material senses are found, upon examination, to be mortally mental, instead of material. Reduced to its proper denomination, matter is mortal mind; yet, strictly speaking, there is no mortal mind, for Mind is immortal, and is not matter, but Spirit.

Force. What is gravitation? Mortal mind says gravitation is a material power, or force. I ask, Which was first, matter or power? That which was first was God, immortal Mind, the Parent of *all.* But God is Truth, and the forces of Truth are moral and spiritual, not physical. They are not the merciless forces of matter. What then *are* the so-called forces of matter? They are the phenomena of mortal mind, and matter and mortal mind are one; and this one is a misstatement of Mind, God.

A molecule, as matter, is not formed by Spirit; for Spirit is *spiritual* consciousness alone. Hence this spiritual consciousness can form nothing unlike itself, Spirit, and Spirit is the only creator. The material atom is an outlined falsity of consciousness, which can gather additional evidence of consciousness and life only as it adds lie to lie. This process it names material attraction, and endows with the double capacity of creator and creation.

From the beginning this lie was the false witness against the fact that Spirit is All, beside which there is no other existence. The use of a lie is that it unwittingly confirms Truth, when handled by Christian Science, which reverses false testimony and gains a knowledge of God from opposite facts, or phenomena.

This whole subject is met and solved by Christian Science according to Scripture. Thus we see that Spirit is Truth and eternal reality; that matter is the opposite of Spirit,—referred to in the New Testament as the flesh at war with Spirit; hence, that matter is erroneous, transitory, unreal.

A further proof of this is the demonstration, according to Christian Science, that by the reduction and the rejection of the claims of matter (instead of acquiescence therein) man is improved physically, mentally, morally, spiritually.

To deny the existence or reality of matter, and yet admit the reality of moral evil, sin, or to say that the divine Mind is conscious of evil, yet is not conscious of matter, is erroneous. This error stultifies the logic of divine Science, and must interfere with its practical demonstration.

Is There no Death?

Jesus not only declared himself "the way" and "the truth," but also "the life." God is Life; and as there is but one God, there can be but one Life. Must man die, then, in order to inherit eternal life and enter heaven?

Our Master said, "The kingdom of heaven is at hand." Then God and heaven, or Life, are present, and death is not the real stepping-stone to Life and happiness. They are now and here; and a change in human consciousness, from sin to holiness, would reveal this wonder of being. Because God is ever present, no boundary of time can separate us from Him and the heaven of His presence; and because God is Life, all Life is eternal.

Is it unchristian to believe there is no death? Not unless it be a sin to believe that God is Life and All-in-all. Evil and disease do not testify of Life and God.

Human beings are physically mortal, but spiritually immortal. The evil accompanying physical personality is illusive and mortal; but the good attendant upon spiritual individuality is immortal. Existing here and now, this unseen individuality is real and eternal. The so-called material senses, and the mortal mind which is misnamed *man*, take no cognizance of spiritual individuality, which manifests immortality, whose Principle is God.

To God alone belong the indisputable realities of being. Death is a contradiction of Life, or God; therefore it is not in accordance with His law, but antagonistic thereto.

Death, then, is error, opposed to Truth,—even the unreality of mortal mind, not the reality of that Mind which is Life. Error has no life, and is virtually without existence. Life is real; and all is real which proceeds from Life and is inseparable from it.

It is unchristian to believe in the transition called *material death*, since matter has no life, and such misbelief must enthrone another power, an imaginary life, above the living and true God. A material sense of life robs God, by declaring that not He alone is Life, but that something else also is life,—thus affirming the existence and rulership of more gods than one. This idolatrous and false sense of life is all that dies, or appears to die.

The opposite understanding of God brings to light Life and immortality. Death has no quality of Life; and no divine fiat commands us to believe in aught which is unlike God, or to deny that He is Life eternal.

Life as God, moral and spiritual good, is not seen in the mineral, vegetable, or animal kingdoms. Hence the inevitable conclusion that Life is not in these kingdoms, and that the popular views to this effect are not up to the Christian standard of Life, or equal to the reality of being, whose Principle is God.

When "the Word" is "made flesh" among mortals, the Truth of Life is rendered practical on the body. Eternal Life is partially understood; and sickness, sin, and death yield to holiness, health, and Life,—that is, to God. The lust of the flesh and the pride of physical life must be quenched in the divine essence,—that omnipotent Love which annihilates hate, that Life which knows no death.

"Who hath believed our report?" Who understands these sayings? He to whom the arm of the Lord is revealed. He loves them from whom divine Science removes human weakness by divine strength, and who unveil the Messiah, whose name is Wonderful.

Man has no underived power. That selfhood is false which opposes itself to God, claims another father, and denies spiritual sonship; but as many as receive the knowledge of God in Science must reflect, in some degree, the power of Him who gave and giveth man dominion over all the earth.

As soldiers of the cross we must be brave, and let Science declare the immortal status of man, and deny the evidence of the material senses, which testify that man dies.

As the image of God, or Life, man forever reflects and embodies Life, not death. The material senses testify falsely. They presuppose that God is good and that man is evil, that Deity is deathless, but that man dies, losing the divine likeness.

Science and material sense conflict at all points, from the revolution of the earth to the fall of a sparrow. It is mortality only that dies.

To say that you and I, as mortals, will not enter this dark shadow of material sense, called *death*, is to assert what we have not proved; but man in Science never dies. Material sense, or the belief of life in matter, must perish, in order to prove man deathless.

As Truth supersedes error, and bears the fruits of Love, this understanding of Truth subordinates the belief in death, and demonstrates Life as imperative in the divine order of being.

Jesus declares that they who believe his sayings will never die; therefore mortals can no more receive everlasting life by believing in death, than they can become perfect by believing in imperfection and living imperfectly.

Life is God, and God is good. Hence Life abides in man, if man abides in good, if he lives in God, who holds Life by a spiritual and not by a material sense of being.

A sense of death is not requisite to a proper or true sense of Life, but beclouds it. Death can never alarm or even appear to him who fully understands Life. The death-penalty comes through our ignorance of Life,—of that which is without beginning and without end,—and is the punishment of this ignorance.

Holding a material sense of Life, and lacking the spiritual sense of it, mortals die, in belief, and regard all things as temporal. A sense material apprehends nothing strictly belonging to the nature and office of Life. It conceives and beholds nothing but mortality, and has but a feeble concept of immortality.

In order to reach the true knowledge and consciousness of Life, we must learn it of good. Of evil we can never learn it, because sin shuts out the real sense of Life, and brings in an unreal sense of suffering and death.

Knowledge of evil, or belief in it, involves a loss of the true sense of good, God; and to know death, or to believe in it, involves a temporary loss of God, the infinite and only Life.

Resurrection from the dead (that is, from the belief in death) must come to all sooner or later; and they who have part in this resurrection are they upon whom the second death has no power.

The sweet and sacred sense of the permanence of man's unity with his Maker can illumine our present being with a continual presence and power of good, opening wide the portal from death into Life; and when this Life shall appear "we shall be like Him," and we shall go to the Father, not through death, but through Life; not through error, but through Truth.

All Life is Spirit, and Spirit can never dwell in its antagonist, matter. Life, therefore, is deathless, because God cannot be the opposite of Himself. In Christian Science there is no matter; hence matter neither lives nor dies. To the senses, matter appears to both live and die, and these phenomena appear to go on *ad infinitum*; but such a theory implies perpetual disagreement with Spirit.

Life, God, being everywhere, it must follow that death can be nowhere; because there is no place left for it.

Soul, Spirit, is deathless. Matter, sin, and death are not the outcome of Spirit, holiness, and Life. What then are matter, sin, and death? They can be nothing except the results of material consciousness; but material consciousness can have no real existence, because it is not a living—that is to say, a divine and intelligent—reality.

That man must be vicious before he can be virtuous, dying before he can be deathless, material before he can be spiritual, is an error of the senses; for the very opposite of this error is the genuine Science of being.

Man, in Science, is as perfect and immortal now, as when "the morning stars sang together, and all the sons of God shouted for joy."

With Christ, Life was not merely a sense of existence, but a sense of might and ability to subdue material conditions. No wonder "people were astonished at his doctrine; for he taught them as one having authority, and not as the scribes."

As defined by Jesus, Life had no beginning; nor was it the result of organization, or of an infusion of power into matter. To him, Life was Spirit.

Truth, defiant of error or matter, is Science, dispelling a false sense and leading man into the true sense of selfhood and Godhood; wherein the mortal does not develop the immortal, nor the material the spiritual, but wherein true manhood and womanhood go forth in the radiance of eternal being and its perfections, unchanged and unchangeable.

This generation seems too material for any strong demonstration over death, and hence cannot bring out the infinite reality of Life,—namely, that there is no death, but only Life. The present mortal sense of being is too finite for anchorage in infinite good, God, because mortals now believe in the possibility that Life can be evil.

The achievement of this ultimatum of Science, complete triumph over death, requires time and immense spiritual growth.

I have by no means spoken of myself, I *cannot* speak of myself as "sufficient for these things." I insist only upon the fact, as it exists in divine Science, that man dies not, and on the words of the Master in support of this verity,—words which can never "pass away till all be fulfilled."

Because of these profound reasons I urge Christians to have more faith in living than in dying. I exhort them to accept Christ's promise, and unite the influence of their own thoughts with the power of his teachings, in the Science of being. This will interpret the divine power to human capacity, and enable us to *apprehend*, or lay hold upon, "that for which," as Paul says in the third chapter of Philippians, we are also "apprehended of [or grasped by] Christ Jesus,"—the ever-present Life which knows no death, the omnipresent Spirit which knows no matter.

Personal Statements

Many misrepresentations are made concerning my doctrines, some of which are as unkind and unjust as they are untrue; but I can only repeat the Master's words: "They know not what they do."

The foundations of these assertions, like the structure raised thereupon, are vain shadows, repeating—if the popular couplet may be so paraphrased—

The old, old story,

Of *Satan* and his *lie*.

In the days of Eden, humanity was misled by a false personality,—a talking snake,—according to Biblical history. This pretender taught the opposite of Truth. This abortive ego, this fable of error, is laid bare in Christian Science.

Human theories call, or miscall, this evil a child of God. Philosophy would multiply and subdivide personality into everything that exists, whether expressive or not expressive of the Mind which is God. Human wisdom says of evil, "The Lord knows it!" thus carrying out the serpent's assurance: "In the day ye eat thereof [when you, lie, get the floor], then your eyes shall be opened [you shall be conscious matter], and ye shall be as gods, knowing good and evil [you shall believe a lie, and this lie shall seem truth]."

Bruise the head of this serpent, as Truth and "the woman" are doing in Christian Science, and it stings your heel, rears its crest proudly, and goes on saying, "Am I not myself? Am I not mind and matter, person and thing?" We should answer: "Yes! you are indeed yourself, and need most of all to be rid of this self, for it is very far from God's likeness."

The egotist must come down and learn, in humility, that God never made evil. An evil ego, and his assumed power, are falsities. These falsities need a denial. The falsity is the teaching that matter can be conscious; and conscious matter implies pantheism. This pantheism I unveil. I try to show its all-pervading presence in certain forms of theology and philosophy, where it becomes error's affirmative to Truth's negative. Anatomy and physiology make mind-matter a habitant of the cerebellum, whence it telegraphs and telephones over its own body, and goes forth into an imaginary sphere of its own creation and limitation, until it finally dies in order to better itself. But Truth never dies, and death is not the goal which Truth seeks.

The evil ego has but the visionary substance of matter. It lacks the substance of Spirit,—Mind, Life, Soul. Mortal mind is self-creative and self-sustained, until it becomes non-existent. It has no origin or existence in Spirit, immortal Mind, or good. Matter is not truly conscious; and mortal error, called *mind*, is not Godlike. These are the shadowy and false, which neither think nor speak.

All Truth is from inspiration and revelation,—from Spirit, not from flesh.

We do not see much of the real man here, for he is God's man; while ours is man's man.

I do not deny, I maintain, the individuality and reality of man; but I do so on a divine Principle, not based on a human conception and birth. The scientific man and his Maker are here; and you would be none other than this man, if you would subordinate the fleshly perceptions to the spiritual sense and source of being.

Jesus said, "I and my Father are one." He taught no selfhood as existent in matter. In his identity there is no evil. Individuality and Life were real to him only as spiritual and good, not as material or evil. This incensed the rabbins against Jesus, because it was an indignity to their personality; and this personality they regarded as both good and evil, as is still claimed by the worldly-wise. To them evil was even more the ego than was the good. Sin, sickness, and death were evil's concomitants. This evil ego they believed must extend throughout the universe, as being equally identical and self-conscious with God. This ego was in the earthquake, thunderbolt, and tempest.

The Pharisees fought Jesus on this issue. It furnished the battle-ground of the past, as it does of the present. The fight was an effort to enthrone evil. Jesus assumed the burden of disproof by destroying sin, sickness, and death, to sight and sense.

Nowhere in Scripture is evil connected with good, the being of God, and with every passing hour it is losing its false claim to existence or consciousness. All that can exist is God and His idea.

Credo

It is fair to ask of every one a reason for the faith within. Though it be but to repeat my twice-told tale,—nay, the tale already told a hundred times,—yet ask, and I will answer.

Do you believe in God?

I believe more in Him than do most Christians, for I have no faith in any other thing or being. He sustains my individuality. Nay, more—He *is* my individuality and my Life. Because He lives, I live. He heals all my ills, destroys my iniquities, deprives death of its sting, and robs the grave of its victory.

To me God is All. He is best understood as Supreme Being, as infinite and conscious Life, as the affectionate Father and Mother of all He creates; but this divine Parent no more enters into His creation than the human father enters into his child. His creation is not the Ego, but the reflection of the Ego. The Ego is God Himself, the infinite Soul.

I believe that of which I am conscious through the understanding, however faintly able to demonstrate Truth and Love.

Do you believe in man?

I believe in the individual man, for I understand that man is as definite and eternal as God, and that man is coexistent with God, as being the eternally divine idea. This is demonstrable by the simple appeal to human consciousness.

But I believe less in the sinner, wrongly named *man*. The more I understand true humanhood, the more I see it to be sinless,—as ignorant of sin as is the perfect Maker.

To me the reality and substance of being are *good*, and nothing else. Through the eternal reality of existence I reach, in thought, a glorified consciousness of the only living God and the genuine man. So long as I hold evil in consciousness, I cannot be wholly good.

You cannot simultaneously serve the mammon of materiality and the God of spirituality. There are not two realities of being, two opposite states of existence. One should appear real to us, and the other unreal, or we lose the Science of being. Standing in no basic Truth, we make "the worse appear the better reason," and the unreal masquerades as the real, in our thought.

Evil is without Principle. Being destitute of Principle, it is devoid of Science. Hence it is undemonstrable, without proof. This gives me a clearer right to call evil a negation, than to affirm it to be something which God sees and knows, but which He straightway commands mortals to shun or relinquish, lest it destroy them. This notion of the destructibility of Mind implies the possibility of its defilement; but how can infinite Mind be defiled?

Do you believe in matter?

I believe in matter only as I believe in evil, that it is something to be denied and destroyed to human consciousness, and is unknown to the Divine. We should watch and pray that we enter not into the temptation of pantheistic belief in matter as sensible mind. We should subjugate it as Jesus did, by a dominant understanding of Spirit.

At best, matter is only a phenomenon of mortal mind, of which evil is the highest degree; but really there is no such thing as *mortal mind*,—though we are compelled to use the phrase in the endeavor to express the underlying thought.

In reality there are no material states or stages of consciousness, and matter has neither Mind nor sensation. Like evil, it is destitute of Mind, for Mind is God.

The less consciousness of evil or matter mortals have, the easier it is for them to evade sin, sickness, and death,—which are but states of false belief,—and awake from the troubled dream, a consciousness which is without Mind or Maker.

Matter and evil cannot be conscious, and consciousness should not be evil. Adopt this rule of Science, and you will discover the material origin, growth, maturity, and death of sinners, as the history of man, disappears, and the everlasting facts of being appear, wherein man is the reflection of immutable good.

Reasoning from false premises,—that Life is material, that immortal Soul is sinful, and hence that sin is eternal,—the reality of being is neither seen, felt, heard, nor understood. Human philosophy and human reason can never make one hair white or black, except in belief; whereas the demonstration of God, as in Christian Science, is gained through Christ as perfect manhood.

In pantheism the world is bereft of its God, whose place is ill supplied by the pretentious usurpation, by matter, of the heavenly sovereignty.

What say you of woman?

Man is the generic term for all humanity. Woman is the highest species of man, and this word is the generic term for all women; but not one of all these individualities is an Eve or an Adam. They have none of them lost their harmonious state, in the economy of God's wisdom and government.

The Ego is divine consciousness, eternally radiating throughout all space in the idea of God, good, and not of His opposite, evil. The Ego is revealed as Father, Son, and Holy Ghost; but the full Truth is found only in divine Science, where we see God as Life, Truth, and Love. In the scientific relation of man to God, man is reflected not as human soul, but as the divine ideal, whose Soul is not in body, but is God,—the divine Principle of man. Hence Soul is sinless and immortal, in contradistinction to the supposition that there can be sinful souls or immortal sinners.

This Science of God and man is the Holy Ghost, which reveals and sustains the unbroken and eternal harmony of both God and the universe. It is the kingdom of heaven, the ever-present reign of harmony, already with us. Hence the need that human consciousness should become divine, in the coincidence of God and man, in contradistinction to the false consciousness of both good and evil, God and devil,—of man separated from his Maker. This is the precious redemption of soul, as mortal sense, through Christ's immortal sense of Truth, which presents Truth's spiritual idea, *man* and *woman*.

What say you of evil?

God is not the so-called ego of evil; for evil, as a supposition, is the father of itself,—of the material world, the flesh, and the devil. From this falsehood arise the self-destroying elements of this world, its unkind forces, its tempests, lightnings, earthquakes, poisons, rabid beasts, fatal reptiles, and mortals.

Why are earth and mortals so elaborate in beauty, color, and form, if God has no part in them? By the law of opposites. The most beautiful blossom is often poisonous, and the most beautiful mansion is sometimes the home of vice. The senses, not God, Soul, form the condition of beautiful evil, and the supposed modes of self-conscious matter, which make a beautiful lie. Now a lie takes its pattern from Truth, by reversing Truth. So evil and all its forms are inverted good. God never made them; but the lie must say He made them, or it would not be evil. Being a lie, it would be truthful to call itself a lie; and by calling the knowledge of evil good, and greatly to be desired, it constitutes the lie an evil.

The reality and individuality of man are good and God-made, and they are here to be seen and demonstrated; it is only the evil belief that renders them obscure.

Matter and evil are anti-Christian, the antipodes of Science. To say that Mind is material, or that evil is Mind, is a misapprehension of being,—a mistake which will die of its own delusion; for being self-contradictory, it is also self-destructive. The harmony of man's being is not built on such false foundations, which are no more logical, philosophical, or scientific than would be the assertion that the rule of addition is the rule of subtraction, and that sums done under both rules would have one quotient.

Man's individuality is not a mortal mind or sinner; or else he has lost his true individuality as a perfect child of God. Man's Father is not a mortal mind and a sinner; or else the immortal and unerring Mind, God, is not his Father; but God *is* man's origin and loving Father, hence that saying of Jesus, "Call no man your father upon the earth: for one is your Father, which is in heaven."

The bright gold of Truth is dimmed by the doctrine of mind in matter.

To say there *is* a false claim, called *sickness*, is to admit all there is of sickness; for it is nothing but a false claim. To be healed, one must lose sight of a false claim. If the claim be present to the thought, then disease becomes as tangible as any reality. To regard sickness as a false claim, is to abate the fear of it; but this does not destroy the so-called fact of the *claim*. In order to be whole, we must be insensible to every claim of error.

As with sickness, so is it with sin. To admit that sin has any claim whatever, just or unjust, is to admit a dangerous fact. Hence the fact must be denied; for if sin's claim be allowed in any degree, then sin destroys the *at-one-ment*, or oneness with God,—a unity which sin recognizes as its most potent and deadly enemy.

If God knows sin, even as a false claimant, then acquaintance with that claimant becomes legitimate to mortals, and this knowledge would not be forbidden; but God forbade man to know evil at the very beginning, when Satan held it up before man as something desirable and a distinct addition to human wisdom, because the knowledge of evil would make man a god,—a representation that God both knew and admitted the dignity of evil.

Which is right,—God, who condemned the knowledge of sin and disowned its acquaintance, or the serpent, who pushed that claim with the glittering audacity of diabolical and sinuous logic?

Suffering from Others' Thoughts

Jesus accepted the one fact whereby alone the rule of Life can be demonstrated,—namely, that there is no death.

In his real self he bore no infirmities. Though "a man of sorrows, and acquainted with grief," as Isaiah says of him, he bore not *his* sins, but *ours*, "in his own body on the tree." "He was bruised for *our* iniquities; ... and with his stripes we are healed."

He was the Way-shower; and Christian Scientists who would demonstrate "the way" must keep close to his path, that they may win the prize. "The way," in the flesh, is the suffering which leads out of the flesh. "The way," in Spirit, is "the way" of Life, Truth, and Love, redeeming us from the false sense of the flesh and the wounds it bears. This threefold Messiah reveals the self-destroying ways of error and the life-giving way of Truth.

Job's faith and hope gained him the assurance that the so-called sufferings of the flesh are unreal. We shall learn how false are the pleasures and pains of material sense, and behold the truth of being, as expressed in his conviction, "Yet in my flesh shall I see God;" that is, Now and here shall I behold God, divine Love.

The chaos of mortal mind is made the stepping-stone to the cosmos of immortal Mind.

If Jesus suffered, as the Scriptures declare, it must have been from the mentality of others; since all suffering comes from mind, not from matter, and there could be no sin or suffering in the Mind which is God. Not his own sins, but the sins of the world, "crucified the Lord of glory," and "put him to an open shame."

Holding a quickened sense of false environment, and suffering from mentality in opposition to Truth, are significant of that state of mind which the actual understanding of Christian Science first eliminates and then destroys.

In the divine order of Science every follower of Christ shares his cup of sorrows. He also suffereth in the flesh, and from the mentality which opposes the law of Spirit; but the divine law is supreme, for it freeth him from the law of sin and death.

Prophets and apostles suffered from the thoughts of others. Their conscious being was not fully exempt from physicality and the sense of sin.

Until he awakes from his delusion, he suffers least from sin who is a hardened sinner. The hypocrite's affections must first be made to fret in their chains; and the pangs of hell must lay hold of him ere he can change from flesh to Spirit, become acquainted with that Love which is without dissimulation and endureth all things. Such mental conditions as ingratitude, lust, malice, hate, constitute the miasma of earth. More obnoxious than Chinese stenchpots are these dispositions which offend the spiritual sense.

Anatomically considered, the design of the material senses is to warn mortals of the approach of danger by the pain they feel and occasion; but as this sense disappears it foresees the impending doom and foretells the pain. Man's refuge is in spirituality, "under the shadow of the Almighty."

The cross is the central emblem of human history. Without it there is neither temptation nor glory. When Jesus turned and said, "Who hath touched me?" he must have felt the influence of the woman's thought; for it is written that he felt that "virtue had gone out of him." His pure consciousness was discriminating, and rendered this infallible verdict; but he neither held her error by affinity nor by infirmity, for it was detected and dismissed.

This gospel of suffering brought life and bliss. This is earth's Bethel in stone,—its pillow, supporting the ladder which reaches heaven.

Suffering was the confirmation of Paul's faith. Through "a thorn in the flesh" he learned that spiritual grace was sufficient for him.

Peter rejoiced that he was found worthy to suffer for Christ; because to suffer with him is to reign with him.

Sorrow is the harbinger of joy. Mortal throes of anguish forward the birth of immortal being; but divine Science wipes away all tears.

The only conscious existence in the flesh is error of some sort,—sin, pain, death,—a false sense of life and happiness. Mortals, if at ease in so-called existence, are in their native element of error, and must become *dis-eased*, disquieted, before error is annihilated.

Jesus walked with bleeding feet the thorny earth-road, treading "the winepress alone." His persecutors said mockingly, "Save thyself, and come down from the cross." This was the very thing he *was* doing, coming down from the cross, saving himself after the manner that he had taught, by the law of Spirit's supremacy; and this was done through what is humanly called *agony*.

Even the ice-bound hypocrite melts in fervent heat, before he apprehends Christ as "the way." The Master's sublime triumph over all mortal mentality was immortality's goal. He was too wise not to be willing to test the full compass of human woe, being "in all points tempted like as we are, yet without sin."

Thus the absolute unreality of sin, sickness, and death was revealed,—a revelation that beams on mortal sense as the midnight sun shines over the Polar Sea.

The Saviour's Mission

If there is no reality in evil, why did the Messiah come to the world, and from what evils was it his purpose to save humankind? How, indeed, is he a Saviour, if the evils from which he saves are nonentities?

Jesus came to earth; but the Christ (that is, the divine idea of the divine Principle which made heaven and earth) was never absent from the earth and heaven; hence the phraseology of Jesus, who spoke of the Christ as one who came down from heaven, yet as "the Son of man *which is in heaven*." (John iii. 13.)

By this we understand Christ to be the divine idea brought to the flesh in the son of Mary.

Salvation is as eternal as God. To mortal thought Jesus appeared as a child, and grew to manhood, to suffer before Pilate and on Calvary, because he could reach and teach mankind only through this conformity to mortal conditions; but Soul never saw the Saviour come and go, because the divine idea is always present.

Jesus came to rescue men from these very illusions to which he seemed to conform: from the illusion which calls sin real, and man a sinner, needing a Saviour; the illusion which calls sickness real, and man an invalid, needing a physician; the illusion that death is as real as Life. From such thoughts—mortal inventions, one and all—Christ Jesus came to save men, through ever-present and eternal good.

Mortal man is a kingdom divided against itself. With the same breath he articulates truth and error. We say that God is All, and there is none beside Him, and then talk of sin and sinners as real. We call God omnipotent and omnipresent, and then conjure up, from the dark abyss of nothingness, a powerful presence named *evil*. We say that harmony is real, and inharmony is its opposite, and therefore unreal; yet we descant upon sickness, sin, and death as realities.

With the tongue "bless we God, even the Father; and therewith curse we men, who are made after the similitude [human concept] of God. Out of the same mouth proceedeth blessing and cursing. My brethren, these things ought not so to be." (James iii. 9, 10.) Mortals are free moral agents, to choose whom they would serve. If God, then let them serve Him, and He will be unto them All-in-all.

If God is ever present, He is neither absent from Himself nor from the universe. Without Him, the universe would disappear, and space, substance, and immortality be lost. St. Paul says, "And if Christ be not raised, your faith is vain; ye are yet in your sins." (1 Corinthians xv. 17.) Christ cannot come to mortal and material sense, which sees not God. This false sense of substance must yield to His eternal presence, and so dissolve. Rising above the false, to the true evidence of Life, is the resurrection that takes hold of eternal Truth. Coming and going belong to mortal consciousness. God is "the same yesterday, and to-day, and forever."

To material sense, Jesus first appeared as a helpless human babe; but to immortal and spiritual vision he was one with the Father, even the eternal idea of God, that was—and is—neither young nor old, neither dead nor risen. The mutations of mortal sense are the evening and the morning of human thought,—the twilight and dawn of earthly vision, which precedeth the nightless radiance of divine Life. Human perception, advancing toward the apprehension of its nothingness, halts, retreats, and again goes forward; but the divine Principle and Spirit and spiritual man are unchangeable,—neither advancing, retreating, nor halting.

Our highest sense of infinite good in this mortal sphere is but the sign and symbol, not the substance of good. Only faith and a feeble understanding make the earthly acme of human sense. "The life which I now live in the flesh I live by the faith of the Son of God." (Galatians ii. 20.)

Christian Science is both demonstration and fruition, but how attenuated are our demonstration and realization of this Science! Truth, in divine Science, is the stepping-stone to the understanding of God; but the broken and contrite heart soonest discerns this truth, even as the helpless sick are soonest healed by it. Invalids say, "I have recovered from sickness;" when the fact really remains, in divine Science, that they never were sick.

The Christian saith, "Christ (God) died for me, and came to save me;" yet God dies not, and is the ever-presence that neither comes nor goes, and man is forever His image and likeness. "The things which are seen are temporal; but the things which are not seen are eternal." (2 Corinthians iv. 18.) This is the mystery of godliness—that God, good, is never absent, and there is none beside good. Mortals can understand this only as they reach the Life of good, and learn that there is no Life in evil. Then shall it appear that the true ideal of omnipotent and ever-present good is an ideal wherein and wherefor there is no evil. Sin exists only as a sense, and not as Soul. Destroy this sense of sin, and sin disappears. Sickness, sin, or death is a false sense of Life and good. Destroy this trinity of error, and you find Truth.

In Science, Christ never died. In material sense Jesus died, and lived. The fleshly Jesus seemed to die, though he did not. The Truth or Life in divine Science—undisturbed by human error, sin, and death—saith forever, "I am the living God, and man is My idea, never in matter, nor resurrected from it." "Why seek ye the living among the dead? He is not here, but is risen." (Luke xxiv. 5, 6.) Mortal sense, confining itself to matter, is all that can be buried or resurrected.

Mary had risen to discern faintly God's ever-presence, and that of His idea, man; but her mortal sense, reversing Science and spiritual understanding, interpreted this appearing as a risen Christ. The I AM was neither buried nor resurrected. The Way, the Truth, and the Life were never absent for a moment. This trinity of Love lives and reigns forever. Its kingdom, not apparent to material sense, never disappeared to spiritual sense, but remained forever in the Science of being. The so-called appearing, disappearing, and reappearing of ever-presence, in whom is no variableness or shadow of turning, is the false human sense of that light which shineth in darkness, and the darkness comprehendeth it not.

Summary

All that *is*, God created. If sin has any pretense of existence, God is responsible therefor; but there is no reality in sin, for God can no more behold it, or acknowledge it, than the sun can coexist with darkness.

To build the individual spiritual sense, conscious of only health, holiness, and heaven, on the foundations of an eternal Mind which is conscious of sickness, sin, and death, is a moral impossibility; for "other foundation can no man lay than that is laid." (1 Corinthians iii. 11.) The nearer we approximate to such a Mind, even if it were (or could be) God, the more real those mind-pictures would become to us; until the hope of ever eluding their dread presence must yield to despair, and the haunting sense of evil forever accompany our being.

Mortals may climb the smooth glaciers, leap the dark fissures, scale the treacherous ice, and stand on the summit of Mont Blanc; but they can never turn back what Deity knoweth, nor escape from identification with what dwelleth in the eternal Mind.

Echo Library

www.echo-library.com

Echo Library uses advanced digital print-on-demand technology to build and preserve an exciting world class collection of rare and out-of-print books, making them readily available for everyone to enjoy.

Situated just yards from Teddington Lock on the River Thames, Echo Library was founded in 2005 by Tom Cherrington, a specialist dealer in rare and antiquarian books with a passion for literature.

Please visit our website for a complete catalogue of our books, which includes foreign language titles.

The Right to Read

Echo Library actively supports the Royal National Institute for the Blind's Right to Read initiative by publishing a comprehensive range of Large Print (16 point Tiresias font as recommended by the RNIB) and Clear Print (13 point Tiresias font) titles for those who find standard print difficult to read.

Customer Service

If there is a serious error in the text or layout please send details to feedback@echo-library.com and we will supply a corrected copy. If there is a printing fault or the book is damaged please refer to your supplier.

CPSIA information can be obtained at www.ICGtesting.com
Printed in the USA
BVOW04s2024060816

458178BV00001B/76/P